Koala bears, lion cubs, pandas, rabbits—these animals are so cute and popular that people everywhere like to buy cuddly, stuffed-animal versions of them and snuggle up to them and put them in special places in their rooms. But that's not true for the creatures in this book. They are so scary or ugly or have such bad reputations that people don't like them much. They are the unhuggables, animals people love to hate.

It's so popular to dislike the creatures in this book that sometimes people don't stop to think before they squash them or run away from them. Sure, you don't want bees landing on a sandwich at the same time you're trying to eat it or grizzly bears ripping into your tent while you're camping. But do you realize that without bees many flowers would not bloom? Do you know that grizzly bears normally avoid people and won't bother you if you know how to behave in grizzly country? Or that only female mosquitoes bite?

As scary or pesty as the animals in this book may seem to you, their lives are fascinating. We hope you enjoy getting to know more about them. If you ever get a chance to see the ones living far away, and the next time you see the familiar ones, maybe you'll have new understanding and respect for them as the wild wonders they are.

National Wildlife Federation

The Unhug

Unwelcome Visitors

Creepy Crawlies

Monsters of the Deep

gables

Blood Lovers

Slimy, Squirmy, Slippery

It's a Snake!

Library of Congress CIP Data: page 95.

Unwelcome Visitors

If a group of wolves, gorillas, skunks, crocodiles, rats, and grizzly bears went trick or treating, they'd scare everybody without wearing any costumes at all! People tend to take one look at these animals and run. They think the creatures are out to crush them, bite them, rip them to shreds, or zap them with a stinky smell. And no wonder. We've all heard the stories about the Big Bad Wolf and about King Kong, the monster gorilla. We've all seen pictures of a crocodile lurking in the water waiting for a canoe to capsize, or of a huge grizzly bear baring its teeth and claws at a hiker. Certainly nobody likes the sight of a rat scurrying through an alley. And if skunks don't look mean, we avoid them because of the nasty scent they spray.

But these reputations are like masks. They keep us from seeing what the animals are really like. If you look behind their reputations, you will discover that these creatures are worth knowing about.

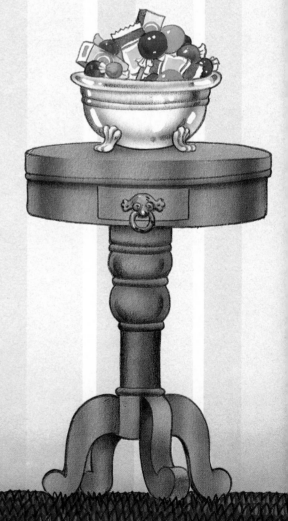

WOLF

Who's afraid of the big, bad wolf? Many people are. Images of hungry wolf packs prowling the woods have frightened people for hundreds of years. Stories like "Little Red Riding Hood" and "Peter and the Wolf" are enough to make anyone want to stay away from forests.

But do wolves really attack people? Very seldom. And of those few attacks, most are probably made by wolves that are injured or infected with rabies. As far as we know, no one in North America has ever been killed by a healthy wolf.

To people who felt their lives and flocks of sheep or herds of cattle were threatened by wolves, the animals became symbols of danger and evil. These symbols are still part of our everyday thought and speech. When we collect food for the poor, we say we are trying "to keep the wolf from the door." The

Wolves are shown as mean villains in cartoons like *The Three Little Pigs* (above) and in stories about Little Red Riding Hood (below). In real life, wolves like the one at right do hunt wild and domestic animals —but they normally leave people alone.

"wolf" here is starvation. And a mean person who pretends to be nice is a "wolf in sheep's clothing."

We still are fascinated by stories of werewolves, people who turn into killer wolves when the moon is full. And legends tell us of children brought up in the woods by wolves. The most famous children were Romulus and Remus, the founders of Rome. Mowgli, the young hero of Kipling's *Jungle Book,* was also raised by wolves. They are wonderful tales, but they are not true.

So, what is the truth about wolves? Wolves look a lot like German shepherd dogs. In fact, wolves and dogs are both canids, a group of animals that also includes foxes, jackals, and coyotes. Gray wolves are the largest of all canids in the wild. A 120-pound male may stretch seven feet from nose to tail.

Wolves are found in every kind of land except dry deserts and wet

jungles. As long as they stay well and find food, and aren't killed by stubborn prey, other wolves, or by people, they live about ten years.

Wolves live in groups called *packs.* A small pack—a half-dozen or so animals—is normally a family. It includes a lead male, his mate, and their young of different ages. Large packs of up to 20 animals include several adults.

Each pack claims an area of land, called a *territory,* where it lives and hunts. The pack drives out any other wolves that enter its territory. Some wolves in southern Canada survive in territories that cover only seven square miles.

Some wolves in Alaska must hunt over an area the size of Connecticut to find enough to eat.

The cries of wolves howling in the night carry for miles in still, cold air. Some people say that wolves howl because they are lonely. Wolves howl for *several* reasons, but we don't know if loneliness is one of them. We do know that wolves hunting over large territories howl to keep in touch with each other. They also howl to warn other packs to stay out of their territory.

Some people picture wolves as fierce hunters that never stop until they catch their prey. Working together, wolves can kill moose and

Hungry wolves, like these eating a deer, gobble down almost every part of their prey, even the fur and bones. Wolves survive by eating animals as small as a mouse and as large as a moose.

other animals much larger than themselves. But they don't succeed at this very often. A single wolf may catch a deer only once every two weeks or so. And a pack usually has to chase 12 moose for every one it brings down.

Between kills, the pack goes hungry, so the wolves must make the most of each catch. A 100-pound animal may "wolf" down 20 pounds of meat in one meal. And it eats almost everything, including the bones and hair.

While the parents hunt, other adult members of a pack sometimes act as babysitters. These "aunts" and "uncles" take care of the wolf pups. If the youngsters get too frisky, the older wolves growl to warn them to behave themselves.

When youngsters in the pack play at fighting, they are trying to settle just who's the boss. Like chickens, wolf packs have a "pecking order," going from the lead male and female at the top down through all members of the pack.

The lead male directs all the activities of the pack. He leads the fight against other wolves that get too close. And he leads the group as it hunts for food. Normally, he is the only male in the pack that breeds. In hard times, only this lead male and other wolves near the top of the pecking order eat well. Those near the bottom get the leftovers, if there are any.

Sometimes a wolf at the bottom of the pack takes off on its own in hopes of finding more food. This wanderer becomes a "lone wolf," hunting alone along the borders between territories. If male and female lone wolves meet, they may mate and form their own pack.

Today, few wolves remain in areas where people live. The last wolves were killed in England 200 years ago. They are rare in Europe outside of Russia. In the western United States, gray wolves were hunted, trapped, and poisoned until they died out about 40 years ago. In the states east of the Rockies, a few packs remain in Minnesota, Michigan, and Wisconsin.

In 1985, a small wolf pack from Canada wandered down into Montana's Glacier National Park. Soon they became the first gray wolves to breed in the West in many years. Not everyone is glad to have the animals back, though. Some people worry because wolves occasionally kill livestock. This happens when the wolves hunt too close to farms and ranches. But in wild areas far from where people live, wolves feed only on natural prey such as deer and elk. Many people hope that the animals will be allowed to return to at least part of their former range.

A wolf pup waits behind while the pack hunts. When the pack returns after a successful hunt, one of the adult wolves spits up bits of meat to feed the cub.

GORILLA

Dino De Laurentiis presents
a John Guillermin Film
"King Kong"
starring Jeff Bridges · Charles Grodin · Introducing Jessica Lange
Screenplay by Lorenzo Semple, Jr. · Produced by Dino De Laurentiis.
Directed by John Guillermin · Music Composed and Conducted by John Barry
Panavision® in Color · A Paramount Release
PG PARENTAL GUIDANCE SUGGESTED
SOME MATERIAL MAY NOT BE SUITABLE FOR PRE-TEENAGERS
Original sound track album and tapes on Reprise Records.

A panicked giant gorilla terrorized the city of New York in the movie *King Kong*. Real gorillas (right) are actually gentle plant-eaters and don't hurt other animals except in self-defense.

African natives called gorillas "wild men of the woods." Early European explorers said the animals were beasts "as awful as a nightmare." Even scientists once believed that gorillas attacked elephants with sticks and kidnapped native villagers. Today, probably only sharks rival gorillas as the ultimate movie monsters. It's easy to see why gorillas fascinate us so much. They look mean and strong enough to fight off any person or animal that gets near them.

But looks are deceiving. Gorillas are shy. They normally move away to avoid danger rather than stand their ground and fight. Because they are plant-eaters, they don't hunt other animals for food. However, if they feel threatened, they put on a show that's sure to scare away almost any intruder.

At first, the strongest male in a group of gorillas makes soft noises, often while sitting down. He starts out calling slowly, then faster and faster and louder and louder. When he stands up, he rips up a nearby bush or breaks a small tree branch and throws it into the air.

Now comes the part gorillas are probably most famous for: chest beating. But the animal doesn't usually use his fist. Instead, he slaps his chest with his open hand. He may also slap his legs or a tree or the back of another gorilla.

If the intruder doesn't leave, the male starts running right at it. At

Grooming helps keep coats clean and free of parasites that carry disease. Often, a gorilla can groom itself. But sometimes gorillas help each other scratch those hard-to-reach places.

the same time he slaps at anything that gets in his way. Suddenly he stops and BAM!—he pounds the ground with his hand.

By now, most animals—and humans—would have run away. Maybe people who did run away made up stories about attacks by killer apes. But scientists who have studied gorillas say that the animals will not harm a person who stays in place. If a person starts to run, though, the gorilla chases him and bites him if he catches him.

One African tribe believes that bites or other injuries from a gorilla attack are marks of shame. The tribesmen say that these injuries are proof the injured person tried to run away like a coward.

George Schaller, a scientist who has spent a lot of time watching gorillas, found another way to keep some gorillas from attacking. He simply looked down and shook his head. Schaller did this whenever he surprised a gorilla in the wild. It was his way of telling the animal, "I mean no harm." Likewise, when he saw a gorilla moving near and shaking its head, he knew that the animal was not going to hurt him.

Scientists have also learned not to stare at gorillas for very long, even through binoculars or cameras. The animals feel threatened when

people stare at them, so they may attack in self-defense.

Normally, gorillas move around in troops. A troop has up to two dozen members and is led by an older male, or "silverback." All older males are called silverbacks because of the silvery hair on their backs. Besides the silverback, a typical troop may have one other adult male, six adult females, and nine youngsters.

A newborn gorilla normally weighs less than five pounds. That's even less than most newborn human babies. But by the time a male gorilla is 12 years old, he may weigh more than 400 pounds. A female weighs about half that much.

Most gorilla troops live in the lowland jungles of western and central Africa, close to the equator. But a few troops survive in and around parks on the wooded slopes of the high mountains where the countries of Zaire, Uganda, and Rwanda come together. The few mountain gorillas that are left are in danger of dying out completely. Some are killed by poachers who sneak into the parks. Others outside the parks die because the places where they live are being destroyed. Each year, more of the jungle is cleared to make places for people to live and grow food.

One day in the life of a troop of gorillas is much like any other day. The animals become active soon after the sun comes up—about 6 a. m. in the tropics. They spend their time eating and searching for more food—usually leaves, fruit, flowers, and roots.

When a gorilla finds a rich source of food, it stuffs food into its mouth with one hand while snatching more twigs and leaves with its other hand. Even the heaviest gorilla will climb a 50-foot tree to reach tasty leaves. But many gorillas refuse to wade through water for any reason.

The silverback sets the pace for the entire troop. When he moves from one feeding area to another, the other animals follow. If he moves slowly, so do the others. If he runs, everyone runs. And if he decides to stop and take a nap, the other animals also stop and rest.

Scientists point out how much gorillas and people behave in similar ways. Gorillas yawn and stretch when they wake up in the morning. When they are undecided about

Gorillas climb cautiously and slowly. Although they spend most of the day on the ground, they occasionally take to the trees to rest, eat, or look around.

Baby gorillas often ride "piggyback," leaving the mother free to move around more easily.

which way to go or what to do, they stop and scratch their heads. People do the same thing at times. Gorillas, and other apes, also express curiosity, anger, jealousy, fear, affection, and pleasure. And, like some human children, young gorillas have temper tantrums when they don't get their own way.

Like people, gorillas catch colds, too. Some of the animals suffer from arthritis. And, sadly, captive gorillas catch pneumonia easily and sometimes die from it.

Gorilla youngsters like to play. They swing on vines, slide down hillsides, and wrestle. If the wrestling gets too rough, a young gorilla "cries uncle" by crouching down and tucking in its arms and legs. The youngsters also play follow-the-leader, going up trees, down vines, across fallen logs, and even over sleeping adults. They keep on playing as they move with the rest of the troop in its search for food.

Members of the troop don't have homes to return to in the evening. Instead, the gorillas settle down wherever they happen to be when the sun goes down. They may bend down some branches in a tree or fold over some bushes on the ground to make a soft place to sleep. But day after day, year after year for 25 to 30 years in the wild, a gorilla's life stays just about the same. Boring? Perhaps—to a human. But to a gorilla, this is the way life is supposed to be.

SKUNK

Adult skunks eat mostly insects and mice, which they catch live (right).

Baby skunks frolic in a field (below) while their mother hunts. They start hunting with her at two months of age. By three months, they are independent of their family and fend for themselves.

When it comes to skunks, there's bad news and there's good news. The bad news is, skunk spray is one of the worst smells in nature. It makes some people and animals sick to their stomachs and can also cause temporary blindness. The good news is, a skunk sprays only in self-defense, and it gives plenty of warning before it does.

Glands at the base of a skunk's tail produce a smelly, oily liquid called *musk*. When a skunk sprays, it forces out the musk in a thin stream like water from a squirt gun. The skunk aims at its victim's face and is accurate up to about 12 feet.

Before it sprays, though, a skunk warns animals—and people—to stay away. The first warning is like a little dance. A skunk arches its back and pats its front feet on the ground. If that warning doesn't work, the skunk shakes its head from side to side. It looks as if it's saying "No!" Finally, the skunk raises its tail and gets ready to spray. Some kinds of skunks stand on their front paws and raise their hind feet in the air to spray. Others stay down on all fours. But the result is the same—stink time.

Gray foxes are among the few enemies that can get past a skunk's defense. A fox on the attack will ambush a skunk and grab its neck, rolling the animal over before it can spray. The fox has to be quick, though. One kind of skunk—the spotted skunk—is so fast it can attack and eat rattlesnakes without being bitten. Usually, skunks eat rodents, insects, eggs, and fruit.

One of a skunk's biggest dangers isn't foxes, though. It's cars. A skunk crossing the road doesn't realize that the pile of chrome, steel, and glass heading toward it isn't another animal. The skunk gets ready to put on its warning act. In a moment it's all over, and the road claims another victim.

If you meet a skunk in the woods, don't panic. A skunk is curious, so it might try to get a closer look at you. Turn and walk away quietly. You are safe as long as the skunk doesn't think you are going to hurt it. But watch out if the skunk starts dancing!

CROCODILE and ALLIGATOR

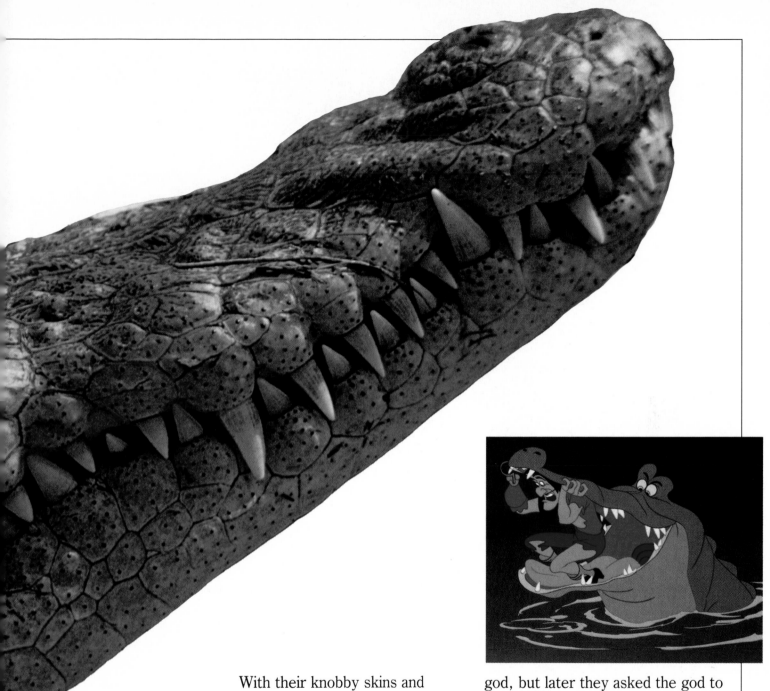

The powerful jaws of the Nile crocodile (above) can crush the bones of cattle and baby hippos. As Captain Hook in *Peter Pan* found out (right), some kinds of crocodiles do attack people.

With their knobby skins and snaggle-toothed grins, crocodiles and alligators sure do look like villains. Even some scientists who study the animals agree. One biologist put it this way: "They're not cuddly. They eat dogs in Florida —sometimes even people. Who could love *them?*"

People have feared and respected these giant reptiles for thousands of years. Ancient Egyptians thought the crocodile was a god. At first they said it was an evil god, but later they asked the god to use its strength to help people in the afterlife. To the Chinese, crocodiles and alligators were powerful dragons. The Chinese gave each year the name of an animal. Anyone born in a "Year of the Dragon" would have power and good luck.

Today, crocodiles and alligators live around the coasts, rivers, and swamps of almost every warm country in the world. The smallest, the Congo dwarf crocodile, is no longer than a yardstick. The

American and Orinoco crocodiles, the largest, grow as long as a large car—more than 20 feet.

How can you tell crocodiles from alligators? Take a look at their snouts. Alligators have broad, rounded snouts. Most crocodile snouts are more pointed. When a crocodile closes its mouth, you can still see some of its bottom teeth sticking up. When an alligator closes its mouth, however, all its bottom teeth are covered.

Both creatures share two impressive features: tough skin and sharp teeth. Their backs are covered with bony scales that protect the animals from most predators. The adults have few enemies besides other crocodiles, alligators, and humans. The young ones, however, are only a few inches long and make easy meals for birds, large fish, or turtles.

The United States has only one kind of crocodile and one kind of alligator. In the U.S., American crocodiles are found only in southern Florida. American alligators are more common. They range from the coast of Texas to the Carolinas. A lot of what we know about American alligators is true of their relatives all around the world.

Teeth and jaws are an alligator's main weapons. With them, it catches fish, frogs, shrimp, snakes, turtles, wading birds, and small mammals. The alligator's teeth are meant for grabbing, not chewing. When it eats, it tears off a mouthful of food and swallows it whole. It also swallows stones to help grind up the food in its stomach.

As you might imagine, an alligator's jaws are very strong. Some clamp down hard enough to crush the bones of a grown cow. But surprisingly, the muscles that open the jaws are weak. A grown man can easily hold the jaws shut with his bare hands. People who wrestle alligators in sideshows understand this, so they are not in as much danger as spectators think—as long as they don't let go.

Though an alligator is a fierce predator, it is a surprisingly gentle parent. Many reptiles abandon their eggs once they are laid. A mother alligator stays near hers for two or three months until they hatch. First, she buries the eggs in a nest made of leaves and grass mixed with sand and mud. Then she stands guard, protecting the nest from raccoons, rats, and other animals that would eat the eggs.

The young alligators face the dangers of hungry fish, birds, and other predators, but the adults don't have it much easier. Their biggest threat comes from people. At one time the problem was over-harvesting—taking too many animals from the wild. Now the problem for alligators is finding a place to live. The places where they thrive are being filled in to make room for everything from homes to shopping malls to golf courses.

If a baby alligator survives to become an 8- to 12-foot adult (right), few animals can threaten it. The much-feared reptiles are quite shy, though, and try to avoid people.

A newly hatched American alligator (below) faces an unfriendly world. Its enemies include birds, snakes, giant frogs, and crabs.

Rats often search for food in garbage (right). Unfortunately, they eat more than just trash. Rats eat or destroy enough of the world's grain each year to feed 130 million people.

Naked and blind, baby rats nurse. Their eyes open in two weeks, and in barely two months they can have babies of their own.

Rats! Just the name makes some people squirm. But should it? Hamsters, gerbils, and mice, which are very popular pets, are members of the rat family. So are more than 1,000 other kinds of small creatures that never do anyone any harm. But black rats, Norway rats, and a few other kinds have caused so much damage and human suffering that they have given all rats a bad name.

Most kinds of rats live in forests or fields, where they eat seeds, nuts, fruits, and sometimes insects. They stay away from where people live. The harmful rats create problems because they adapt so well to living around farms and cities. Rats like the same foods people do, so whatever people grow, rats try to eat. Asian rats eat enough rice each year to feed half the people in India.

Rats in a chicken coop can be as destructive as hungry foxes. They may kill the chickens and eat the eggs. Rats aren't always afraid of large animals, either. In one German circus, rats bit the feet of three elephants so badly that the animals died from infection.

Some scientists think that rats have killed more people than all the wars in history. The deaths were caused by diseases the rats carry. About 600 years ago, black rats brought the bubonic plague to Europe from Asia. The plague germs lived inside fleas that lived on the rats. When the fleas bit people, the people got sick. Before it was over, the plague killed nearly a third of the people in Europe.

Rats are not as dangerous as they once were. Doctors now have medicines to treat many of the diseases that rats may carry. Even so, no one wants to get bitten. The worst problems with bites happen when rats move into dirty buildings in which garbage is lying around.

Getting rid of rats is not easy. If poisoned bait is put out, rats won't eat enough to kill them. Instead, they nibble just a little bit and wait to see if it makes them sick. If it does, they leave the rest alone. Scientists developed a poison that takes a long time to make the rats sick. The idea is that the rats would be fooled into thinking the poison was safe to eat. That worked for a while. But rats reproduce so quickly that new "super rats" have evolved that are immune to this poison.

Some people have turned the tables on these pests by using healthy rats for food. Rat meat is as nutritious as beef and chicken. One company in the Far East canned rat meat under the brand name STAR —which is "rats" spelled backwards.

Scientists like rats because their body organs work very much like human organs. Companies test new foods and medicines on white Norway rats. If the rats get sick, the products are probably not safe for people to use. As one scientist put it, "Few people have not benefited by studies made on the rat."

GRIZZLY BEAR

This sign in Yellowstone National Park warns hikers to be careful because the trail leads through an area where grizzlies have been seen.

A full-grown grizzly like the one at right weighs 800 pounds or more and can run faster than a horse.

It seems that people have always had strong feelings about grizzly bears. To some western Indian tribes, the grizzly was a sacred creature. Yosemite, one of America's most spectacular national parks, got its name from an Indian word meaning "grizzly bear." The Indians that did hunt grizzlies proudly wore necklaces made of bear claws as proof of bravery.

Grizzly bears also impressed the early explorers and settlers in the American West. When Lewis and Clark explored that area in 1804-1806, they got their impressions of the bears at very close range: a grizzly chased Meriwether Lewis right into the Missouri River.

Today, many people admire grizzlies because they are so big and strong. Yet many other people see the grizzly as a dangerous threat. They point out that the bears occasionally attack hikers and campers or raid ranches to kill sheep and cattle.

At one time, grizzlies roamed the western mountains and plains from Mexico to Alaska. As more and more people moved into areas where the grizzlies lived, more and more bears were killed. South of Canada, probably fewer than 900 grizzlies remain—in Montana, Idaho, Wyoming, and Washington.

If you ever saw a newborn grizzly, you might find it hard to believe that someday it would be big enough to kill cattle or moose. Baby grizzlies are so small it would take five cubs together to weigh as much as one newborn human baby. But full-grown grizzly males can be real giants. They weigh anywhere from 300 to more than 1,000 pounds. They can also run up to 30 miles per hour. That's twice as fast as a runner doing a four-minute mile.

The largest grizzly bears live along the coast of Alaska and British Columbia. They are often called "brown bears" instead of grizzly bears. But scientists give both kinds the name *Ursus arctos,* which means "northern bear."

One way to tell a grizzly from other bears is by the hump over its shoulders. This hump is filled with muscles that power the bear's front legs. With these muscles—and also with their three-inch-long claws— grizzly bears dig for roots and for mice and other creatures.

Grizzlies belong to a large group of animals called "carnivores," a word that means "meat-eaters." But these bears probably eat more plant food than anything else. In the spring they eat grass, roots, moss, and bulbs. Later in the year they add fresh berries to their diet.

The bears do eat meat when they can get it. They feed on everything from mice and ground squirrels to moose.

Though grizzly bears cannot see well, they have a keen sense of smell. An Indian saying puts it this way: "A pine needle fell. The eagle

Mother grizzly bears like the one at left nurse their cubs for about five months. The young bears stay with her for up to three years.

When not feeding on salmon, grizzly bears make a meal of almost anything edible—from honey, fruit, and berries to ground squirrels, grass, and garbage.

saw it. The deer heard it. The bear smelled it."

If a grizzly picks up the scent of a human, it usually takes off in the opposite direction. But on rare occasions a grizzly has attacked a camper or hiker in the Rocky Mountains. The danger is greatest in unsettled areas—especially Yellowstone and Glacier national parks.

Why do the bears attack people? Usually for one of three reasons: the bears are females defending their cubs; the bears have been surprised and are defending themselves; or they are hungry and think the people are carrying food.

There are ways for people to protect themselves from grizzlies. The first rule is to avoid the bears altogether. Hikers should make

noise so the bears know they are coming. Bears usually avoid people. Campers should keep their food sealed and away from their tents. The smell of food attracts bears.

Sometimes a charging bear will stop the attack and back up. Don't run. Try to walk to a tree you can climb and go up at least ten feet. Adult grizzlies seldom climb trees. "Stay in the tree until the bear is gone," one biologist advises, "even if that means roosting all night."

If grizzly bears are so dangerous, why should we want to save them? They are part of this country's wildlife heritage. One biologist describes them as symbols of the wilderness: "We look at them with fear *and* respect and say that they deserve to live, too."

Creepy Crawlies

Get it off me! Stomp on it! Kill it! Isn't this what most people say when they see the creatures we call *creepy crawlies*?

It's hard to avoid some of these little animals. They seem to pop up at the very worst times. A walk through the woods might lead you right into a sticky spider web. Or a family of cockroaches might decide that *your* kitchen is the perfect place to have *their* breakfast. And who wants to see a big fat millipede crawling out of his shoe?

Creepy crawlies are often pests. Some bite and sting, and some are poisonous. But they are also very interesting. Have you ever noticed that some kinds of spiders *don't* spin webs? Do you know how a centipede can run without tripping over its own legs? Creepy crawlies are small, but in fascinating ways they manage to survive very well in a large and often unfriendly world.

SPIDERS

The red "hourglass" tells us this spider is a female black widow. Its poison is 15 times stronger than the venom of a rattlesnake.

A tarantula, like the one at right, can't see very well and it doesn't have ears. But the tiny hairs covering its body detect vibrations from the movements of both enemies and prey.

A jewelry store in San Francisco has new guards on the night shift. They don't carry guns. They're so small that when they patrol the store, they do it *inside* the jewelry cases. Sound unbelievable? Not if the guards are the giant spiders called *tarantulas*.

It's not hard to imagine why tarantulas got the job. They have needle-sharp fangs and a reputation for biting people. They also have hairy legs that can spread out wide enough to cover this page. Seeing one would scare most anyone away.

But wait. The jewelry store owners are playing a trick on burglars. Common North American tarantulas aren't all that dangerous. They *don't* bite people, except in self-defense, and their bite doesn't hurt any more than a bee sting. They have such a gentle disposition, in fact, that some people keep them as pets. Tarantula owners who let their pets crawl up their arm do have to watch out, though: tarantula toes can tickle! And some of the spiders have hairs that give people a very bad rash.

Many people think tarantulas and other spiders are great. In some countries, spiders are symbols of patience and good luck. In the tropics, the huntsman spider is a welcome house guest because it eats cockroaches and other pests.

Four hundred years ago in England, doctors used spiders for medicine. Have a fever? Swallow a spider wrapped in bread crumbs, they said. One doctor, Dr. Thomas Muffet, admired spiders so much he let them run all around his house.

But many people *don't* think spiders are great. Take Dr. Muffet's daughter, Patience, for example. She was the real Little Miss Muffet. We all know from the nursery rhyme that she must not have picked up any of her father's love for the creatures.

What is it about spiders that brings out the shivers? Is it fear of their bite? Perhaps. But of the 30,000 kinds of spiders in the world, only a dozen or so are dangerous to people.

People living in North America need to watch out for only two kinds of spiders—"widows" and brown recluses. The black widow, the most common widow, is shiny and black and has a pea-sized abdomen. The underside of the abdomen usually bears a red spot shaped like a tiny hourglass. The brown recluse is brown to yellow and has a violin-shaped mark on its body.

Both kinds of spiders usually stay in out-of-the-way places. They are shy and back away when disturbed—if they can. Sometimes the widow hangs out inside shoes, on the lids of trash cans, even under the seats of outhouses. The brown recluse can sometimes be found in undisturbed clothing, behind furniture, and in storage sheds. If cornered or pressed against someone's

Will this spider get caught in its own web? Probably not. Strong claws and legs hold its body clear of the sticky spirals, and a coat of oil on its legs helps keep them from getting stuck.

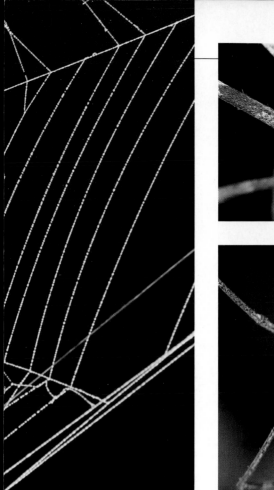

This web-casting spider tosses its web to snag beetles and ants at night. If the web gets torn or worn, the spider bundles it up and eats it at dawn.

skin, the widow and the recluse do what most spiders do in self-defense. They bite.

A bite from either a widow or a recluse can make a person very sick. On top of that, a bite from a recluse can turn into a large, deep sore that may take months to heal. Fortunately, few people die from one of these bites if they get medical treatment right away.

But it can't be just the thought of poison that makes some people afraid of spiders. In England, where Little Miss Muffet lived, there are no poisonous spiders at all.

So what else could bring out the shivers? The web? The hairy body?

The thin, scurrying legs? It's hard to say. But we do know this. Despite their scary features, most spiders are *not* dangerous to people.

For insects, other spiders, even small birds and snakes, however, spiders are *very* dangerous. The very features that may scare us—webs, legs, and bites—help make spiders clever, successful hunters.

Some spiders, like the garden spider, weave a beautiful web and dribble sticky glue along the spiraling silk threads. They build these thin nets between stalks of grass, the branches of bushes, even in windows or doorways, and wait for insects to crash into them.

Unlike most spiders, the jumping spider (right) has keen eyesight. In nine leaps out of ten it lands right on its prey.

A small fish makes a big meal for this fishing spider (below). Usually the spider catches only tiny insects.

Not all webs are like nets stretched across an open space. The hammock spider covers bushes with tangled mats that look like thin carpets of cotton candy. But these webs are not sticky. They don't have to be. Insects that light upon the mats trip over the threads and can't move fast enough to get away.

Then there is the web-casting spider. First, it spins a small, elastic web that is strong and sticky. Next, holding the web in its four front legs, it hangs upside-down close to the ground. When an insect trots by underneath, the spider opens the net and spreads it over what will probably be its next meal.

The bolas spider makes one of the strangest of all traps. At dusk, the spider hangs from a single, thin strand of silk. It makes another strand with a sticky, round glob on the end. The spider sends out a "perfume" that imitates the scent of a female moth. When a male moth looking for a mate approaches, the spider swings its sticky glob like a bolas and ZAP! snags its meal.

Not all spiders spin webs. Some stalk, pounce, or even fish for their food. These spiders often rely on strong, swift legs. A wolf spider roams over the ground until it detects, say, a nearby millipede. It stops. Then slowly, silently, it stalks. Finally, when close enough, it pounces. Jumping spiders are the master pouncers, however. Some jump up to 40 times their length.

A fishing spider sits on water plants and rests its front legs on the surface of the water. When it feels the ripples made by insects or small fish, it scoots across the water and scoops out its next meal.

No matter what the style of attack, almost all spiders have one thing in common—poison. The poison helps the spider eat and digest its food by turning the inside of the prey's body into soup. When the "soup's done," the spider uses its strawlike mouth to suck it up.

Poison also quiets down struggling prey. A spider can't risk a long fight. It might get so tired the prey can escape. Worse still, a long struggle could attract the attention of a bird or frog or other hungry enemy. For a spider, poison can make the difference between *having* a meal and *being* one.

A fire ant locks its jaws onto its victim's skin, then swings the back end of its body around to sting again and again.

Imagine this. You sit down under a tree to have a picnic. Before you know it, little ants are crawling over your food, across your jeans, and up your arms. You jump up, brush them off, and move to another spot.

Common, pesky ants like these do no real harm. But one kind of ant now spreading across the United States is downright destructive and dangerous. This is the fire ant.

Fire ants *look* like most any other ant, but to any creature that crosses their path, they are mini-monsters that attack with both ends of their body. With sharp, powerful jaws they bite into their victim's skin and lock on. Then they sting with a stinger on their back ends. Any ant that is not pulled off stings

again and again. This sting feels like being poked with a red-hot needle and gives the fire ant its name.

When fire ants sting their prey —small creatures like earthworms and centipedes—one sting is often enough. When they attack anything larger, it is usually in self-defense —even if the "enemy" has done nothing more than get too close. Then one sting is rarely enough.

Fire ants have been known to attack and kill small animals like birds, mice, and pigs. They rarely kill humans, though each year fire ant bites make 10,000 people sick enough to visit a doctor.

Fire ants are not native to the United States. They arrived in the 1940s as accidental hitchhikers on

Red-suited mascots of the Marshall, Texas, Fire Ant Festival join an over-sized "anteater" as part of an annual event that attracts crowds of tourists.

cargo ships from South America. For these new arrivals, the southern United States turned out to be a perfect place to set up new homes: plenty of flat, open fields and *no* enemies.

In just forty years, fire ants have spread from Alabama into Texas and North Carolina. Their nests are mounds of dirt and are as hard as concrete and as much as three feet high and three feet across. These mounds have ruined millions of acres of farmland.

Farmers and government experts have tried to control the fire ant with pesticides. But few sprays reach far enough inside the mounds to kill all the ants hiding there.

Besides, many of the pesticides killed a lot of the native wildlife—squirrels, birds, and other insects. It may be years before a safe, effective control is found.

Meanwhile, at least one town is trying to make the best of a sore situation. Every October, townspeople turn out for the Fire Ant Festival in Marshall, Texas. They dress up for the Fire Ant Costume Contest, jitterbug through the Fire Ant Stomp, and compete in the Fire Ant Calling Contest. Will fire ants really come when called? Probably not. Ants don't have ears. But that doesn't keep anyone from having a good laugh over fire ants—at least for a couple of days.

Hundreds of fire ants may nibble on this dragonfly before it is completely gone. When the ants return to their nest with bits of food, they leave a chemical trail that leads other ants to the feast.

WASP and BEE

Bzzzzzzt! Have you heard the good news about bees and wasps? Only the females can sting. A bee's or wasp's stinger has to double as a tube for laying eggs. And since males don't lay eggs, males don't have stingers. The bad news is that most bees and wasps you see or hear are females! Most of the males live only a few days, just long enough to mate.

Don't worry too much about getting stung, though. Bees and wasps have better things to do than buzz about looking for people to attack. Honeybees and bumblebees spend their days visiting flowers to gather nectar and pollen. Yellow jackets, hornets, and paper wasps—all members of a wasp family—cruise about looking for juicy caterpillars and crunchy spiders. They carry these creatures back to the nest to feed their hundreds or thousands of hungry, growing youngsters.

Did you ever get the feeling a wasp was following you? Or did you ever have a bee buzzing around your head? They were probably just looking for food. Yellow jackets love jelly sandwiches and soda pop. Bees will check out anything with bright colors and sweet smells—even if that "flower" turns out to be a person wearing a colorful shirt and perfume or after-shave.

Stinging is often more dangerous for a wasp or bee than it is for the people or animals being stung.

Worker wasps bring small bits of caterpillar back to the nest to feed to their growing larvae, or young wasps.

39

A quick slap can turn one of these tiny attackers into a flat splat. For a honeybee, slap or not, a sting means certain death. When the bee stings, tiny hooks hold the stinger firmly in the victim's skin. Then when the bee flies away, its stinger and part of its abdomen tear loose and stay behind. The sting may only hurt the victim, but it kills the bee.

Sometimes you can tell if a bee or wasp is going to sting. In warm weather, beehives and hornet nests give off a soft, steady *hummmmm.* That is the sound of hundreds of workers fanning the hive with their wings to keep it cool. If the humming changes to a loud, angry *buzzzzz,* the creatures are angry and upset and ready to attack.

One kind of bee doesn't hesitate to sting and doesn't give warnings. The slightest disturbance sends them boiling out of their nest to attack any creature in sight. Scientists call them "Africanized bees" because they are a cross between mean-tempered African honeybees and gentle European honeybees. Other people call them "killer bees" because they have killed rabbits, cows, chickens, and even people.

A killer bee's sting is no worse than the sting of other honeybees. It's just that killer bees are much more fierce. They attack by the hundreds without warning. They defend larger areas than other bees do, making it dangerous to get within 100 yards of their nest. (That's the length of a football field.) The swarm also chases and stings victims for an hour or more, even after the animal or person has run a long way from the bees' nest.

Killer bees, brought to South America for scientific study, es-caped from a lab in Brazil in 1957. Since then, they have moved northward at a rate of about 200 miles a year. Scientists predict that the bees will spread through the southern United States by the 1990s.

A sting from a wasp or bee hurts, no doubt about that. And thoughts of killer bees are certainly scary. But most of the time when you hear a wasp or a bee, you can go your way and they will go theirs.

If you have just hit a high fly into a hornet's nest or stepped on the underground nest of a bumblebee colony, you'll probably see or hear several angry buzzers heading straight for you. *Run!* Wasps and bees fly at more than 15 miles per hour—faster than you could run—so you may get a sting or two. But once you get a few yards away, the attacks will stop.

If the buzzes come from wasps or bees out on their daily food run, your safest move is not to move at all—even if a wasp or bee lands on your arm. Try a light wave of your hand or a gentle puff of breath to tell it, nicely, to "buzz off" and look somewhere else for food.

In a "bee beard" contest, the man at left attracted thousands of bees to his face by putting a queen bee in a cage tied to his chin. He also used young worker bees that are much less likely to sting.

Pollen sticks to a bee's knees and the rest of its body when it pokes into flowers for food. Spreading pollen from flower to flower helps the plants make seeds.

SCORPION

Sometimes scorpions capture prey, like this grasshopper, without having to sting. But they keep their tails curved forward, ready to use if their dinner fights back.

There's no denying that a scorpion looks scary and dangerous. Its two powerful pincers can tear apart spiders, centipedes, and cockroaches. The curved stinger at the end of its long, curled tail can strike with lightning quickness and kill small snakes and lizards in seconds.

But most people in North America have little to fear from scorpions. Any scorpion will attack in self-defense, but the sting of most is no more painful than a bee or wasp sting. Only a few kinds have poisons that are strong enough to kill people. These kinds live in Arizona and Mexico. The dangerous stings can be treated—but people

"There I was! Asleep in this little cave here, when suddenly I was attacked by this hideous thing with five heads!"

All aboard! For their first week of life, baby scorpions ride on their mother's back. If one falls off, mom will often look for it and help it climb on again.

A drop of venom hangs like dew from this scorpion stinger. For humans, the sting of most scorpions is no worse than a bee sting.

still get very sick. So, if you're in a hot, dry climate where scorpions live, *watch where you step* and know where scorpions hide—under rocks, under loose bark, even inside shoes that are left outside overnight.

The story of scorpions includes more than pincers and poison. Did you know that scorpions "listen" with their feet? Whenever animals move around, they make the ground or whatever they are walking on vibrate. Scorpions have hairs on their feet and slits on their ankles that detect these vibrations. By "listening" this way, a scorpion can tell where the other creature is, how big it is, and whether it is an enemy, a mate, or a possible meal.

For most of their lives, scorpions live by themselves. Oc-casionally, in cool weather, several may huddle together under a rock. And, of course, they come together to mate. But usually when scorpions meet, they fight to the death—and the winner eats the loser.

The only other time scorpions stay together is when they are babies. Just after they're born, baby scorpions climb onto their mother's back. Even then, they stay for only a short time. After about a week they drop off and live on their own.

As soon as their legs touch the ground, the youngsters get their first "look" at the world around them. Vibrations tell them it is an exciting world filled with other creatures. Some of the vibrations mean food, some mean enemies, and others mean future mates.

COCKROACH

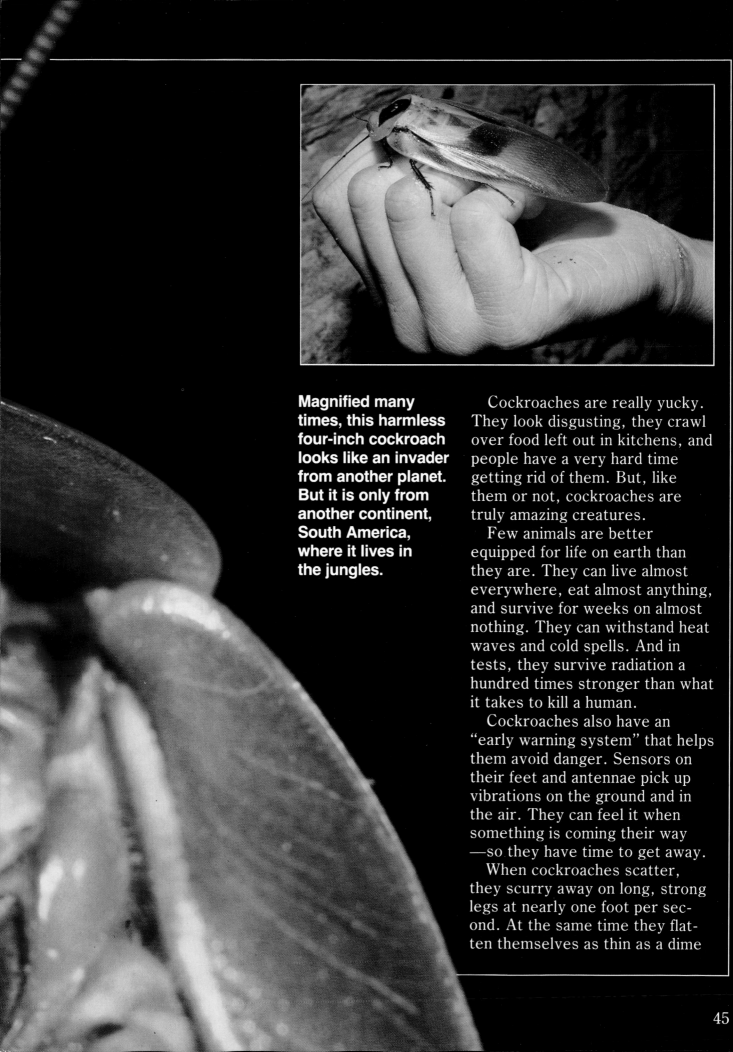

Magnified many times, this harmless four-inch cockroach looks like an invader from another planet. But it is only from another continent, South America, where it lives in the jungles.

Cockroaches are really yucky. They look disgusting, they crawl over food left out in kitchens, and people have a very hard time getting rid of them. But, like them or not, cockroaches are truly amazing creatures.

Few animals are better equipped for life on earth than they are. They can live almost everywhere, eat almost anything, and survive for weeks on almost nothing. They can withstand heat waves and cold spells. And in tests, they survive radiation a hundred times stronger than what it takes to kill a human.

Cockroaches also have an "early warning system" that helps them avoid danger. Sensors on their feet and antennae pick up vibrations on the ground and in the air. They can feel it when something is coming their way —so they have time to get away.

When cockroaches scatter, they scurry away on long, strong legs at nearly one foot per second. At the same time they flatten themselves as thin as a dime

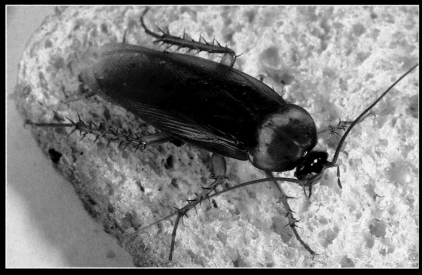

Cockroaches nibble on nearly everything, from bread (above) to wallpaper paste. A few kinds can eat wood, and some are cannibals, eating other cockroaches.

and squeeze to safety through cracks and crevices. Cockroaches are so successful at staying alive that they have survived for more than 350 million years—since before the age of dinosaurs.

Today, nearly 4,000 kinds of cockroaches populate the earth. Most live in warm tropical forests. But some also live in deserts, grasslands, and swamps —every place on earth except the polar regions. Some live under bark, leaves, and stones. Some burrow in the ground, and some live in caves. Others live in nests of ants, wasps, and ter-

mites. Some Asian cockroaches spend part of their lives in water.

German, Oriental, and American cockroaches are the most familiar kinds in North America. These creatures thrive in all kinds of buildings—apartments, homes, hospitals, stores, restaurants—any place they can find warmth, moisture, shelter, and plenty to eat. Some even turn up on ships and submarines.

Cockroaches are creatures of the night. By day, they hide in walls, cupboards, sewers, under floorboards, and even inside microwave ovens and computers.

Under cover of darkness, cockroaches come out to eat. They love food with lots of sugar, protein, and oil. In addition to the food people eat, their diet includes Vaseline, shoe polish, and—one of their favorites —soap. They also eat paper, wool, leather, dead animals, and the glue in the bindings of books.

As they creep across countertops, dishes, and food, they leave behind foul droppings as well as a trail of germs that rub off their feet. There is no proof that cockroaches spread diseases. But the germs they carry can cause diarrhea and infections.

Obviously, cockroaches are not going to win any prizes in a popularity contest. Instead, humans have dedicated themselves to wiping out the pests. But that's a tough job. Once in a building, cockroaches are usually there to stay. It is hard to find a poison strong enough to kill all the cockroaches, yet safe enough to use around people. And cockroaches quickly learn to avoid places where poison has been set out. If just one pair of cockroaches survives, they and their offspring can produce 100,000 cockroaches in only one year.

So, how should you cope with these "perfect insects" if you spot them where you live? You can start by wiping the counters, cleaning the drains, and emptying the garbage frequently. And you can put away all the leftovers when you're finished eating. You can also call the exterminator.

Soon, North Americans may have yet another night visitor to deal with—the Asian cockroach. Unlike the other kinds of cockroaches, the Asian ones do not scurry away and hide when you turn on the light. They may even fly over to greet you.

Asian cockroaches were first spotted in Florida in the mid-1980s. Will people be able to stop them from spreading? Probably not. Birds and snakes and frogs and lizards may eat some of them. But the rest are expected to spread along the East Coast to New Jersey and up the West Coast to Washington state.

Newly hatched Malaysian cockroaches (above) spread out from their egg case. As they scatter, they search for food by night and hide under leaves and stones by day.

Most cockroaches come in shades of brown. A few are pale green. Some, like these Southeast Asian cockroaches, have bright stripes or spots of black, yellow, and red.

CENTIPEDE and MILLIPEDE

The very names *centipede* and *millipede* tell you how creepy and crawly these creatures are. In Latin, "centipede" means "one hundred feet" and "millipede" means "one thousand feet." Well, no centipede has exactly 100 legs. And the name "millipede" is a great exaggeration. But to someone who doesn't want to take a close-up look, the number of legs may look like a million.

With so many legs, how do these creatures keep from tripping over their own feet? Thanks to studies made with high-speed cameras, scientists now have some of the answers.

On most centipedes, each pair of legs is slightly longer than the pair just before it. This way, any pair of legs can slide right out from under the pair behind it and be ready to take another step. Some kinds of centipedes, however, have legs that are all quite short and are seldom used for walking. These centipedes move more like earthworms. They use their legs as anchors to keep from slipping backwards as they stretch their bodies forward.

Even the fastest centipedes can't always outrun hungry birds and lizards and other predators. So they use their legs in other ways. One kind of centipede drops one of its legs when it is chased. This loose leg keeps wriggling around, distracting the predator while its owner gets away. Another kind of centipede gives off drops of sticky glue when it is in danger. Then it uses its legs to flick these drops at its enemies and slow them down.

Like most millipedes, this forest floor millipede of South America is secretive and slow moving. It is active mainly at night.

A millipede is much slower than most centipedes and its walk is more complicated. Its legs move like little ocean waves—some going up, some going down, some up, some down, all the way from head to tail. When the millipede runs, these waves move quickly. When the millipede burrows in the ground, the waves are slow.

Are centipedes and millipedes dangerous to people? Not usually. A centipede gives a poisonous bite with its strong fangs. But this bite is usually used to capture prey or fight off enemies. Most centipedes can't bite through human skin. At worst, the bites of the centipedes found in the United States feel like the stings of yellow jackets. Tropical centipedes, which are up to 10 inches long, are more dangerous. Their poisonous bites cause fever and leave painful swelling that can last for three weeks.

Millipedes don't have a dangerous bite, but they spray a strong chemical for self-defense. Some tropical millipedes can hit their enemies from nearly three feet away. The spray irritates small animals but it comes out in amounts too small to hurt humans.

Sometimes, however, farm workers accidentally dig into groups of millipedes feeding around the roots of the crops. If the workers chop up too many of the little creatures, they may get sick from breathing all the spray given off.

Whether looking for food (above) or protecting their eggs and young (below), centipedes often make use of their poisonous bite.

Monsters of the Deep

Are you ever afraid when you go into the ocean? If so, have you ever stopped to ask yourself just what you're afraid of? Is it the grasping tentacles of an octopus? Do you picture the tooth-filled jaws of huge sharks or killer whales lurking just beneath the surface, waiting to attack you?

People have always feared monsters that supposedly lived in the sea. Storytellers still scare us with tales of giant octopuses and man-eating sharks. Many of these stories are exaggerated. Some are completely made up. So, why do people believe them so easily? Perhaps because sharks and octopuses look weird and frightening. And perhaps because a few kinds of sharks *are* very dangerous—though they seldom attack swimmers along America's shoreline. After you read this chapter, *you* decide if any of these creatures really are monsters of the deep.

OCTOPUS

Eight grasping arms make an octopus look like a spooky monster. But these sea creatures are really shy. They normally crawl along the ocean floor (right). Suckers on their arms (below) help them capture crabs and other creatures.

An octopus looks like a creature straight out of a Halloween horror story. It has a big head in the middle of eight long arms dotted with hundreds of round, rubbery suckers. Many people believe that the suckers suck blood out of victims, including humans. They also think that octopuses grab swimmers and pull them under water. But these people are wrong. Don't let octopuses scare you. They are one of the shyest animals in the sea.

Most octopuses have bodies no larger than a grown man's fist. Even the largest bodies are only about the size of footballs. But the long arms make the animals seem much larger. Arms of an average octopus stretch barely two feet from tip to tip. The arms of Pacific octopuses, the largest in the world, may reach fifteen times that size.

Only one kind of octopus is deadly to people. Called the blue-ringed octopus, it lives in the western Pacific from Australia to southern Japan. This little creature has arms barely three inches long. Like most other octopuses, it is shy and usually crawls away from people. But if picked up or stepped on, it bites—and injects saliva so poisonous it can kill a grown man in a very short time. The saliva of all octopuses is poisonous, but only that of the blue-ringed octopus can kill people. Scientists say this octopus is one of the most poisonous creatures in the sea.

Octopuses use their poisonous saliva to paralyze crabs and other sea creatures they eat. The saliva can turn a crab's flesh almost into a liquid, making it easier for the octopus to suck it out of the shell.

Each of an octopus's eight arms has about 240 suckers, which are round, muscular suction cups. The largest suckers are just over two inches across. The smallest are less than half the diameter of a pencil. One scientist said that suckers feel

like "hundreds of tiny wet, clammy hands pulling at the skin."

An octopus uses these suction cups to hold on to crabs, clams, shrimp, and other prey. Although the suckers are small, together they create a very tight grip. One skin diver tried playing tug-of-war with an octopus, pulling one end of a pole to take it away from an octopus holding on at the other end. The diver did not succeed.

An octopus also tastes with its suckers. It can tell the difference between salty, sweet, and bitter foods. In fact, octopus suckers are more sensitive to taste than the human tongue.

Although an octopus's suckers are strong, its arms are not very tough. Sharks, moray eels, and other animals that eat octopuses twist or bite off the arms easily. But that doesn't seem to bother the octopus. It apparently doesn't feel any pain. And later it grows back its missing arm.

Sometimes an octopus eats its own arms. Why? No one knows for sure, but it seems to happen only if the octopus is sick and about to die.

If you ever see an octopus bleed, you'll notice that its blood is blue. That's because a copper compound in its blood turns it that color. (An iron compound makes human blood red.) The blood is circulated by three hearts. Two send blood to the gills to pick up more oxygen. The third pumps the fresh blood through the octopus's body.

Octopuses have different ways to get away from eels, sharks, seals, and other enemies. Sometimes they squirt out an octopus-sized blob of ink. When the enemy attacks the ink, the octopus swims to safety.

Sometimes octopuses escape through small openings in the reefs where they live. Getting through a narrow spot is no problem. An octopus just sticks in one arm, flattens itself out, and pulls itself through. Scientists have watched octopuses a foot long squeeze through holes an inch across.

At the same time, an octopus may change its color to match its surroundings. Being a quick-change artist helps it hide even when escape holes are not handy. Cells of different colors cover an octopus's body just under its thin, colorless skin. The octopus can make these cells large or small in a fraction of a second. One moment the animal may be a reddish brown. The next it may be speckled or colorless.

Octopuses seem to be deaf. But deafness may help rather than hurt the animals. Some whales that eat octopuses make loud noises to stun their prey. Being deaf may help octopuses withstand these attacks.

The only truly dangerous octopus, the Pacific blue-ringed octopus lives in the western Pacific Ocean. This six-inch-long creature carries enough venom to kill ten people.

It may be hard to think of them as some of nature's best mothers, but female octopuses take very good care of their eggs. A scientist watched one guard hundreds of eggs for more than two months. She squirted water over the eggs almost constantly to clean them.

Octopuses continue to surprise people. Some fishermen discovered that the animals were handy for recovering sunken treasure. The men wanted to pull up some valuable old pots in a sunken wreck. So, they tied strings to octopuses and lowered them near the wreck. The octopuses crawled into the pots and held on as the men pulled them, treasure and all, to the surface.

Octopus eggs hang in strands, guarded by the mother. She constantly squirts water over them to keep them clean. Young octopuses grow inside the eggs for about six weeks, then push themselves out and swim away.

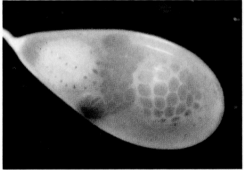

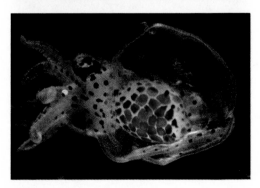

SHARK

In the movie _Jaws_, a great white shark cruises the shoreline hunting for humans to devour. The real great white (right) prefers to eat marine mammals, fish, sea turtles, and birds. When this shark does attack people, it probably mistakes them for seals or dolphins.

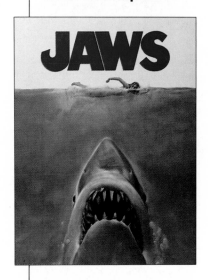

If you had to pick the scariest creature in the sea, what would you choose? A shark? Most people probably would, especially if they had seen the movie or read the book _Jaws_. Sharks really do look scary. Some have as many as 3,000 teeth, and stories of attacks on people make front-page news. But do sharks hurt people very often, and do they hunt humans for food?

Around the whole world, only about 100 shark attacks are reported each year. If you think of how many people swim and fish in the ocean, that's not very many attacks. Most of them occur off the coasts of Africa, South America, Asia, and Australia. The United States reports only about 12 shark attacks annually—and 600 cases of people being struck by lightning.

Even though shark attacks are rare, swimmers and divers should know the best ways to avoid them. Sailors need to know how to protect themselves if their boats sink or they fall overboard at sea. One expert advises divers never to dive alone and never to swim in an area where sharks have been spotted.

Scientists have tried using chemicals, streams of air bubbles, and electricity to drive sharks away. But nothing seems to work all the time. Some of these efforts repel one kind of shark but attract others. Hotel owners along Australian coasts where sharks were a menace found one method that works for

sure. They put up strong, shark-proof nets around the beaches.

Scientists think that some shark attacks on people may be accidents. The shark is not trying to catch its dinner. Instead, it is defending itself because it thinks it is in danger. Almost any shark—and there are more than 350 kinds—will attack if it feels threatened.

All sharks get a bad reputation because of the attacks of a few. Only four kinds are dangerous enough for scientists to call them "man eaters." These are the mako, the tiger, the hammerhead, and the great white shark, probably the best-known of all.

The great white shark often appears as the "bad guy" in books and movies. Some of what is written about this animal is true, but a lot is exaggerated. In size, this shark is "great," often measuring 20 to 25 feet long. That's longer than an average living room. But it doesn't develop a taste for human flesh. It normally feeds on seals and dolphins. Attacks on people probably happen because the shark mistakes them for its usual prey.

Like most other sharks, the great white depends primarily on its sense of smell to find food. In fact, two-thirds of a shark's brain deals with smells. Scientists say that a shark can smell one drop of blood in 25 gallons of water.

Mako sharks, close relatives of the great white, are among the

Most sharks, like the horn shark above, are no threat to people. Horn sharks eat small sea urchins and shellfish that they find on the shallow ocean bottom. Twisted folds of skin on the shark's nostrils (right) help it detect faint odors of food.

long as great whites, but they have enormous appetites. They even attack fierce crocodiles where rivers enter the sea. Stranger still, some tiger sharks have been found with cardboard boxes, license plates, and paint cans in their stomachs—apparently the result of feeding on garbage thrown into the water.

Of all the sharks in the seas, hammerheads are probably the strangest looking. With their wide, flat snouts they do look a little bit like living, swimming hammers.

Over the years, scientists have tried to learn what the shark's wide "hammer" is useful for. Does having its eyes so far apart give the shark better vision for seeing prey? Does the wide shape make the shark more streamlined, letting it move more easily through water? Does having its nostrils far apart help the shark locate its prey by smell?

Scientists now think that electricity is the answer. Hammerheads and other sharks can detect weak electric currents, the kinds produced by the nerves in an animal's body. This sensitivity lets a shark home in on its prey's natural electricity. A wide snout gives the hammerhead room for an extra-large detection system.

Although the four man-eating sharks get most of the publicity, other sharks can be just as extraordinary. Megamouth, a close relative of the predatory great white shark, is about as long as a small car. But even with its 400 teeth, this giant will not harm swimmers. It filters its food from the water. When this shark swims in the ocean's dark depths, its huge mouth glows in the dark, attracting tiny shrimp and other small creatures.

fastest fish in the world. One was clocked at more than 60 miles per hour. Mako sharks normally hunt schools of fish in the open seas. They avoid the shallow water close to shore, so they pose little threat to swimmers. But they have been said to attack people who fall overboard from ships.

Tiger sharks do swim close to shore when they search for crabs, sea lions, stingrays, and other food. As a result, they have been a problem along warm beaches in all parts of the world. They are not as

At more than 50 feet long, whale sharks are the largest fish in the world. Like the megamouth shark, they don't bite humans. These giants feed by swimming slowly and filtering plankton from the water. They also hang vertically in the water with their heads just beneath the surface. When waves pass by, they bob up and down and fill their mouths with fish.

Lemon sharks, which eat mostly fish, are unusual in the shark world because they can rest on the ocean floor. Many sharks have to swim all the time to keep oxygen-filled water flowing over their gills, but lemon sharks don't. They have special muscles that pump water over their gills while they rest. But it is hard work. Lemon sharks use less en-ergy to breathe when swimming than when lying on the ocean floor.

Horn sharks are another "safe" shark. They are often seen in public aquariums. These slow-moving, three-foot-long sharks normally feed on the ocean floor. There they pick up crabs, lobsters, and clams and crush them with their flat back teeth.

Sharks really have more to fear from people than people do from sharks. We use their rough skin for leather and sandpaper, their teeth for ornaments, their oil for vitamin supplements, even parts of their eyes for human transplants. In the Far East, soup made with shark fins is a popular dish. And in England, the "rock salmon" sold in fish and chips shops is really shark.

A breaking wave on the coast of Mexico reveals a chilling sight: a lemon shark that has ventured close to shore, probably in search of food. Luckily, lemon sharks rarely attack people.

KILLER WHALE

What should you think of a whale called "killer"? The name suggests that this creature is mean and vicious. Eskimos used to tell stories about killer whales breaking through ice to knock hunters into the water and eat them. In the early 1960s, a U. S. Navy manual warned divers that killer whales "attack human beings at every opportunity."

Yet killer whales now are popular entertainers in aquariums such as Sea World and Marineland. They leap through hoops, they snap fish gently from their trainers' hands, and they carry their trainers on their backs as they swim and dive. Are these whales killers or not?

To begin with, killer whales are big. A large male measures 30 feet long and weighs 9 tons—longer and heavier than any animals that live on land, even elephants.

Where do they live? A joking reply might be, "Anywhere they want to." Killer whales are found in every ocean, but most of them live along the coasts in the cooler parts of the world. They are regularly seen along the coast of Washington state and adjacent British Columbia. They live in groups called *pods*. Some pods stay in the same areas year-round. Other pods migrate, probably following food supplies.

These pods seem to stay together for life—which is about 50 years for a male and up to 100 years for a female. As one scientist put it, "The only way a pod member arrives or leaves seems to be by birth or death."

When out of sight of each other, members of a pod keep in touch by making short, high-pitched cries. At other times they generate sounds that resemble whistles and clicks. Scientists are not sure what the whistle sounds are for. The clicks seem to work like sonar to help the whales home in on their prey.

Killer whales got their nickname because they are the world's largest predator of warm-blooded animals— a large category that includes seals and dolphins in addition to other whales. But being predators of large animals doesn't make these whales "killers" any more than frogs are "killers" because they eat insects.

When killer whales go fishing, all adult members of the pod work together to round up the prey. The whales often follow schools of salmon, herding the fish close to shore and trapping them there. Then the whales pick off all they want to eat.

If a killer whale spots a penguin or other prey sitting on a piece of floating ice, it wages a different kind of attack. First it dives, then rushes upward, hitting the ice and knocking its prey into the water.

Do the whales attack people on ice the same way? Probably not. Scientists now have spent nearly 20 years studying the animals, and they say there is not a single documented case of killer whales attacking and killing human beings.

Killer whale mothers nurse their calves for up to a year. A baby whale will remain with the same pod, or group of whales, for its entire life.

Blood Lovers

Blood milkshake, anyone? You probably think this sounds disgusting, but some creatures would love to slurp one down.

Few things make a person's skin crawl more than an animal that dines on blood, especially human blood. It's hard not to shiver at the thought of a vampire bat's bite or at the discovery of a tick stuck on your arm or leg.

In spite of our fears, blood-loving animals don't usually hurt people. Ticks, fleas, and mosquitoes can spread serious diseases, but most of them living in the United States do not. Bats can spread rabies, but they very seldom bite people. Leeches may send you running in disgust from a swimming hole, but they rarely cause any real harm to people.

It may come as a surprise to you, but some leeches are helpful to doctors performing difficult operations. Like bees, some kinds of bats help pollinate flowers. So perhaps it's worthwhile to find out a bit about *all* these creatures—from a distance, if you prefer.

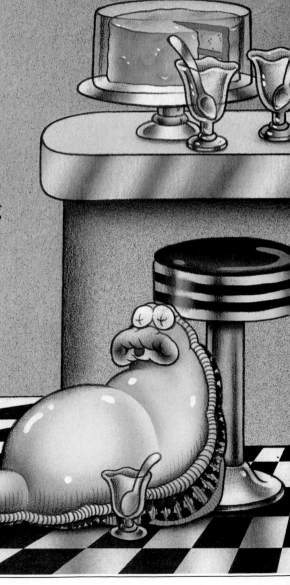

VAMPIRE BAT

Each evening at dusk, as most creatures are settling down to sleep, most bats are just waking up. Out they burst from caves, tunnels, old wells, abandoned buildings, and roosts in trees. Alone or in groups of tens and hundreds, even thousands, they fly the night skies looking for dinner. Most dart after insects. Some fly from tree to tree in search of fruit, nectar, and pollen. Others snap up small lizards, frogs, mice, or fish. Vampire bats, found from Argentina to southern Mexico, search for much bigger animals—chickens, pigs, even cattle and horses. How do these bats, the size of chipmunks, eat such large ani-

mals? They don't. They drink their blood.

Years ago, hungry vampire bats had to search high and low in thick forests to find birds, capybaras, tapirs, or deer. Today, large areas in the forests have been cleared of trees and turned into farms and ranches. The bats now cruise over open pastures and weedy fields where they often come upon farm or ranch animals—a "fast food" stop for vampire bats. With more food available and easier to find, the number of bats has increased in recent years.

One by one the vampire bats land. They look like large, hairy spiders as they scurry across the

Hardly bigger than a mouse, this three-inch-long vampire bat feeds on the foot of a chicken. Unlike the make-believe vampire Dracula (above), the bats rarely bite humans.

ground and over their animal hosts, looking for a spot to bite. When a bat finds a good spot, it gives a couple of licks with its long tongue and makes a quick, small cut with its razor-sharp teeth. Blood oozes out and the bat begins to drink.

Let's get one thing straight. A vampire bat doesn't *suck* blood. It *licks* it, *laps* it, or *sips* it. A chemical in the bat's saliva keeps blood from clotting. So, the cut made by a vampire bat continues to ooze blood as long as the bat keeps licking.

Both cutting and feeding are painless, so the sleeping animal doesn't even wake up. One or two tablespoons of blood a night is about all a vampire bat can drink, so one visit from a vampire bat is not likely to kill or even injure an animal. The real danger comes from a disease some of the bats spread, rabies. Fortunately, very few vampire bats—or any other bats—carry this disease.

There is one problem with a liquid diet, even in small amounts. It's heavy. A tiny but hungry bat may double its weight in one sipping. After a meal like that, it may be too heavy to fly for a while.

What do vampire bats do when they're not sipping blood? They hang out—upside down—in their roost. They scratch some. They groom some. Little bat babies

hang onto bat mothers and nurse some. But mostly the bats just hang there, digesting their meal and sleeping.

A diet of blood is very unusual among bats. Most bats—more than 700 of them—eat insects and other creepy crawlies. Some, like the heart-nosed bat, perch on low branches and wait for dinner to scurry by on the ground below. Others fly around trees and bushes looking for insects and spiders sitting on the leaves.

Most insect-eating bats catch their dinner "Red Baron style," swooping down on prey in midair. Some snap up insects with their mouths. The acrobatic red bat

Sharp, pointed teeth help the vampire bat slice a neat, circular hole in its victim. The bat then laps up the blood as it oozes from the wound.

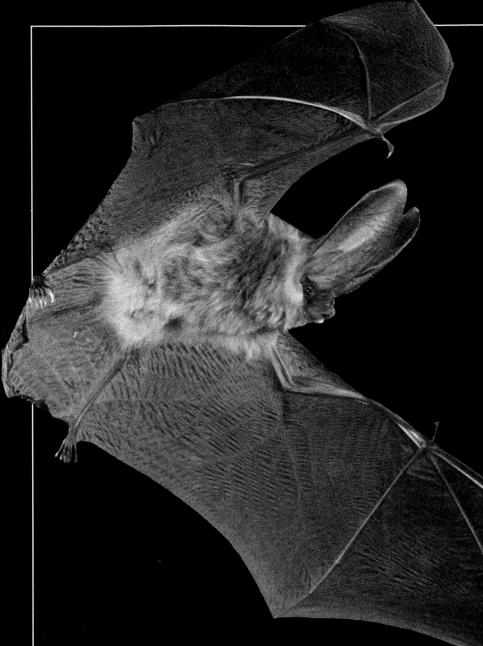

Gentle and shy nectar-eaters, fruit bats roost during the day, hanging upside down (right).

The big-eared bat, like most bats, is not a blood lover. As it flies at night, it uses its large, sensitive ears to detect the insects it eats.

one summer. At this rate, bats are one of the best controls of insects. As people all over the United States and Europe learn this, they build bat houses to invite bats to dinner—right in their back yards.

Many bats eat fruit or nectar and pollen. These bats are a big help to trees and other flowering plants. Fruit bats often serve as freight planes. The bats carry undigested plant seeds to new places and drop them to the ground, mixed with their waste material. Some of the seeds grow. Nectar feeders help carry pollen from one flower to another—an important trip because male pollen has to mix with female flowers before some trees can produce seeds.

Some people are afraid of bats. They think, incorrectly, these little creatures will swoop down to attack them and get tangled in their hair. These people don't know the real bats—shy creatures that go out of their way to avoid people. And when bats eat, they are actually doing us some favors—pollinating flowers, spreading the seeds of trees, and snapping up pesky gnats or mosquitoes that might otherwise end up buzzing around our heads.

can scoop up an insect with its wings, turn a somersault in the air as it pops the insect into its mouth, and unfurl its wings again in time to pull out of the dive.

When bats eat insects they do it in a big way. How about 150 mosquitoes for dinner? A little brown bat eats that many in 15 minutes! A colony of 50 million Mexican free-tailed bats can eat 13 million pounds of insects in

This leech will swell as it sucks blood from a human arm (above). Leeches come in different shapes and colors. The striped leech below may take six months to digest one blood meal.

The year was 1985. The doctor at Children's Hospital in Boston had a problem. A few days earlier, he had operated on a little boy whose ear had been bitten off by a dog. The doctor sewed the ear back on, but now too much blood was building up around the ear, keeping it from healing. To avoid more surgery, the doctor turned to an unusual but safer treatment: leeches. He placed a hungry leech on the boy's ear, and soon the creature began to suck out all the unwanted blood. The ear was saved.

People have used the blood-eating worms known as leeches to treat ailments for hundreds of years. They once thought that letting leeches suck out "bad" blood would cure headaches, fevers, and other diseases. We now know that the real effect of this bleeding is just the opposite. Losing blood makes people weaker—and sicker.

The doctor in Boston used his leeches for a purpose that really works: removing excess blood from wounds. A leech can drink up to 11 times its weight in blood. Once it has filled up, however, a leech may not eat again for a year. So several leeches may be needed to keep such an injury healing properly.

Leeches look scary, but using them for an operation is safe and painless. The kind of leech a doctor might use measures between two and five inches long. Like other leeches, it holds on with suckers at both ends of its body. One end has a mouth with three tiny jaws and hundreds of teeth. Once the leech is in place, the teeth saw back and forth to make a Y-shaped cut for feeding. Chemicals in the leech's saliva seem to deaden any pain and also keep the blood flowing.

Do most leeches live on blood? Yes, but several of the larger kinds

eat or feed on small creatures such as snails and other leeches.

The popular image of leeches shows them lurking in swamps, marshes, lakes, ponds, and slow streams. And that is just where most leeches do live. A researcher in Illinois once discovered 10,000 leeches in an area measuring barely three feet on a side. That's about the size of the top of a card table.

The smallest leeches are less than a half-inch long. The largest, the giant Amazonian leech of South America, is more than a foot long. It lives in marshes and feeds on the blood of snakes and turtles as well as of cattle that come to the water to drink.

Terrestrial leeches—those that live on land—also turn up in many parts of the world. Scientists have found one kind in the American midwest. They say it lives in damp soil, where it eats worms.

The kinds of leeches doctors in the United States use live in Europe and North America. Today, the demand for leeches in medicine is small, but increasing. For a long time, the best way to collect the creatures was to wade through a marsh and pull off the ones that stuck to your legs. Now a scientist has made raising them a successful business. He keeps the leeches in buckets and fish tanks, feeding them blood from slaughterhouses.

A horse leech swims in search of food. Not a blood-sucker, this leech eats tiny animals like worms and insect larvae, which it swallows whole.

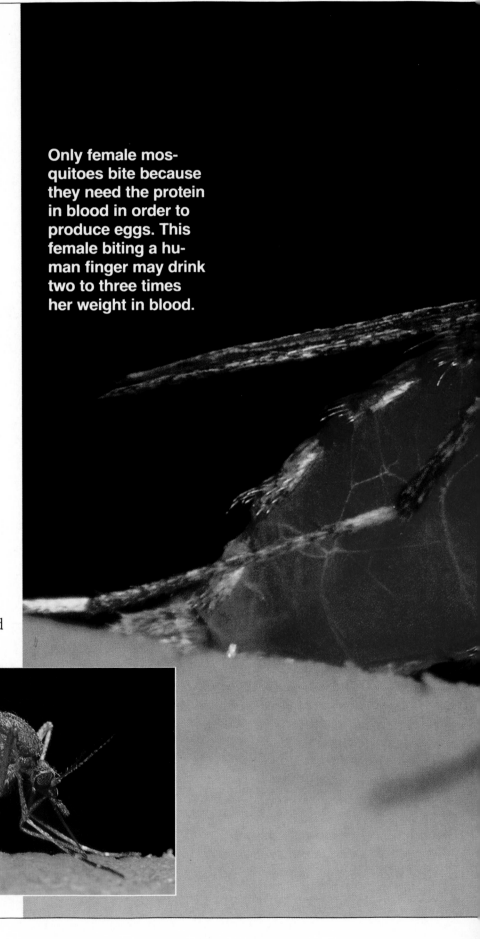

MOSQUITO

How can creatures so small be so deadly? That's what many people ask when they hear mosquitoes called "some of the most dangerous animals in the world." After all, anyone can swat the little pests. Mosquitoes are so light it takes 10,000 of them to weigh an ounce. You probably wouldn't know when one landed on you except for its itchy bite. That bite is what makes these insects so dangerous.

In some places, the mosquitoes' saliva carries germs that cause painful and even fatal diseases. In the early 1800s, most of Napoleon's army in the Caribbean died of yellow fever spread by mosquitoes. This disaster forced Napoleon to give up trying to control most of the land France owned in the New World. He eagerly sold the French territories west of the Mississippi River at a very low price, about four cents an acre. That sale was the famous Louisiana Purchase—and mosquitoes helped make it happen.

Only female mosquitoes bite because they need the protein in blood in order to produce eggs. This female biting a human finger may drink two to three times her weight in blood.

Female mosquitoes are the ones that bite and spread disease. They need blood for their eggs to develop. The males eat nectar from flowers and juices from fruit.

Hungry mosquitoes have no trouble finding their victims. They detect the carbon dioxide that animals—and people—give off when they breathe. Holding your breath wouldn't help keep mosquitoes away, though. They can also detect body heat, sweat, and odor.

When the female is ready to feed, she stabs her sharp feeding tube through the skin and into a

Mosquito larvae (right) hatch from eggs laid on the water's surface (above). Fish often eat the larvae.

blood vessel. Saliva flows into the wound to keep the blood flowing, then the mosquito starts sucking. A minute or two later, filled with two or three times her weight in blood, she takes off. Animals and people are left to scratch the spots where the saliva makes them itch.

How can mosquitoes be stopped from spreading diseases? One step is to eliminate the places in towns and cities where disease-carrying mosquitoes breed near people. These places range from water-filled tree stumps to abandoned tires.

Another way to stop the mosquitoes is to kill mosquito larvae before they develop into adults. The insecticide called DDT got rid of a lot of larvae, but it also killed birds and other animals. The search goes on for safer insecticides.

In some places, people rely on natural predators to eat the larvae. Mosquitofish have been used for this purpose from rice fields in California to the Lincoln Memorial's reflecting pool in Washington, D.C.

In 1985, the United States was invaded by a new danger, Asian tiger mosquitoes. They were first noticed in Texas inside old, wet tires imported from the Far East. Since then, they have turned up from California to Maryland.

What makes these mosquitoes so dangerous? Several things. They seek out humans for their blood. Their bites leave sores. Their eggs survive freezing, so the mosquitoes can spread into the cold northern states. They also resist many poisons that kill other mosquitoes.

But the worst danger lies in the way these mosquitoes spread disease. Normally, mosquitoes pick up disease germs only from sick peo-

ple. If a mosquito carrying germs doesn't bite a human being, the germs die when the mosquito dies. But these new mosquitoes can pass the germs on to their own offspring. Even if a tiger mosquito dies without making anyone sick, its offspring will get another chance.

People can fight back, though. They can pick up discarded cans, jars, buckets, tires—anything that might hold rainwater where mosquitoes breed. And they can turn their backyards into good homes for birds, frogs, toads, and any other animals that love to eat mosquitoes.

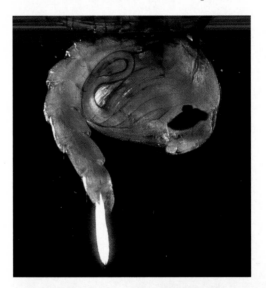

An adult mosquito (below) emerges from its pupa (left) like a butterfly coming out of its cocoon. Until its wings harden, the mosquito cannot fly and can easily be caught by spiders, fish, and other enemies.

TICK and FLEA

A tick waits for its next meal on a fern (above). When a person or animal brushes by, the tick latches on and digs its head into the skin. As the tick feeds, it swells with blood, as this dog tick has done (right).

Ticks and fleas are not related, but the little pests have a lot in common: They both bite, they suck blood, they spread disease, and in general they make life miserable for people and animals.

Ticks may be the most patient creatures on earth. Some hang on to bushes for up to two years waiting for animals to brush against them. Other ticks have survived in scientists' laboratories for more than 20 years without eating.

In woods and fields, ticks hang on to bushes and grass with their fourth pair of legs. They wave their first pair around to detect the heat of passing animals. Some kinds of ticks also have eyes and can tell the difference between light and dark. When a shadow passes over one of these ticks, the tick reaches out for whatever's coming. If the shadow belongs to a deer or other animal, the tick grabs hold and bites.

Rows of sharp, barbed teeth cover part of a tick's lower lip. These barbs stick into the skin and hold on like fishhooks. In addition, the tick's saliva acts as a natural glue. When this glue hardens, it helps hold the tick in place.

Scientists call ticks an animal's worst enemy. Ticks spread painful and often deadly diseases to both wild and domestic animals. Ticks also rank second only to mosquitoes as carriers of diseases that affect people. Rocky Mountain spotted fever, tularemia, Lyme disease—

these are just a few of the illnesses people get from ticks.

Fleas don't have to hang around and wait for rats or cats, foxes or dogs, or people to brush against them. When a flea's senses say GO!, the creature *jumps*. In almost no time it is latched onto a warm body, ready to eat.

When fleas land on their hosts, they grab hold and start sucking blood. A hammerlike bar inside the flea's head pounds away to poke a tiny hole through its host's skin. This sounds painful, but the animal or person barely notices it.

When the host starts scratching, fleas are ready to take off in a hurry. In a good jump, a flea may leap a foot into the air—not bad for an insect barely an eighth of an inch long. That's equal to a grown man jumping almost the length of two football fields.

How can fleas jump so far? They have a secret catapult. Before jumping, a flea pulls up its hind legs and squeezes them tightly against pads of strong rubberlike material on its abdomen. Little hooks hold each leg in position. When ready to leap, the flea unhooks its legs and SNAP! The pads spring back, force the legs down, and launch the flea into the air. It's all automatic, and the flea doesn't seem to get tired. Scientists watched fleas jump hundreds of times an hour for several days without stopping.

In the wild, fleas attach themselves to animals like this rabbit (above) and live on their blood. In captivity, some fleas are put to work as entertainers. Hitched to small carriages (below), they perform in a flea circus.

Slimy, Squirmy, Slippery

Could you hug a slug? or a worm? or a slimy eel? Probably not. Some creatures look so yucky that many people don't want to touch them. But just because these creatures aren't warm and furry and cute doesn't mean we should ignore them.

Slime is disgusting to us, but worms and slugs and eels can't get along without it. Without slime, eels would lose their ability to stay alive out of water and slugs would have a hard time moving from place to place. You might not choose a worm for your favorite animal, but worms help us all by fertilizing and breaking up the soil as they burrow in the ground. These creatures may be ugly, but they are worth a second look.

SLUG

To a slug, a ripe strawberry (right) means a tasty dinner. To a gardener, the slug is a pest that eats prized fruits and vegetables.

At least one slug has its defenders. These California basketball players picked the banana slug to be their team symbol. Here they sport yellow sweatsuits and antennae to match their colorful mascot perched on the basketball.

Sliding on slime may not seem like an ideal way to travel, but to a slug it's the only way to go. Slime, or mucus, oozes from its whole body and forms a shimmering carpet for the slug to slide forward on. The carpet protects the slug's foot as it crawls across even the roughest surfaces. Long after a slug has passed, its carpet remains—silver streaks across sidewalks, through grass, up tree trunks.

Mucus on a slug does more than just provide a smooth highway. Some slugs with lots of mucus can slip from the grip of a hungry predator. Mucus on all slugs also makes it possible for the slug to get almost half the oxygen it needs. By keeping the body moist, it allows the slug to breathe through its skin.

Another kind of mucus holds two slugs together so they can mate. Most slugs mate on the ground, but some only mate while hanging from tree limbs or walls on thick, twisting strands of slime.

Slugs occasionally eat earthworms or other slugs, but they are vegetarians at heart. Tomatoes, beans, carrots, even strawberries are some of their favorites—much to the dismay of farmers.

Not everyone thinks of slugs as hungry pests or mucus makers. Early German and French settlers in North America caught slugs, soaked them in vinegar to remove their slime, sauteed them in butter and garlic, and *ate* them!

Today, scientists are studying slugs to get ideas about building computers. Simple as its brain may be, the slug can do two things that computers can't do—yet. Slugs can learn. They can also "think" about several things at once. Computers wired like a slug's brain could solve problems up to a million times faster than today's computers.

Students at the University of California at Santa Cruz are really fond of slugs—but not to eat. They picked the big, bright yellow banana slug to be their school mascot. While the real banana slugs are sliming around outside under redwood trees, hoop-shooting "Slugs" are dribbling down the basketball court to cheers of "*Go,* Sluggos! Slime 'Em! Slime 'Em!"

WORM

As the earthworm burrows in the soil, it eats decaying plants and animals and leaves little piles of waste called castings at the top of its tunnel. Castings are rich in nutrients that help fertilize the soil.

Everyone knows earthworms. An earthworm may very well have been the first animal you picked up and played with. When you pull one out of the soil or pick one up off a wet sidewalk, the soft, slimy creature wriggles all over the palm of your hand.

Worms are soft and slimy, all right. But if you had X-ray vision to watch them in their natural habitat —under rocks or leaves or deep in their damp underground burrows —they would not be wriggly. In-

stead, they would be crawling slowly along. First, by stretching the front of its body forward, a worm becomes long and skinny. Then, by pulling the back of its body up to the front, it becomes short and fat. A moving worm looks a little like an accordion being played very slowly.

An earthworm wriggles when it is exposed to the sun and dry air. It can't stand being dry! An earthworm breathes through its skin, and its skin must be moist to breathe.

After a few minutes out of the ground, it has trouble breathing and it also starts to lose the water in its body. It wriggles to reach the safety of the moist, dark earth.

There's no way an earthworm could win a mucus-making contest against a slug or an eel. But mucus is very important for earthworms. Mucus makes it easier for earthworms to slide through rough soil and under sharp rocks. It protects earthworms against infection. And it holds two earthworms together when they mate.

One kind of mucus smells awful and may scare away enemies. Another is applied to the walls of burrows, where it dries like concrete and keeps them from caving in.

The earthworm just might win a contest of numbers and size, however. Earthworms are found all over the earth—anywhere green plants and moist soil exist. The only places they can't live are deserts, which are too dry, and polar regions, which are too cold. But in many soils, as many as *seven million* worms may live in an area the size of a football field. And in Australia, one kind of earthworm grows to a length of twelve feet.

Earthworms are good news to plants—and to the many, many animals that eat earthworms. Earthworm burrows are beneficial, too. Crisscrossing every which way and going as deep as eight feet, they serve as expressways for water and

air to reach plant roots, fungi, bacteria, and ants.

Earthworms also make our world a better place to live—by eating it. Worms feed on rotten leaves and other parts of decaying plants. They also eat tiny organisms such as bacteria that live on the surface of sand and bits of clay.

To an earthworm, decaying materials are nuggets of nutrition. Some of this food turns into energy or makes the earthworm grow bigger. The rest of it, along with the extra soil, passes through the worm and becomes waste. You probably have seen these wastes, but didn't know it. They are the little wriggly piles of damp soil in gardens and under grass leaves. Called *castings,* they are rich in fertilizer because the earthworm has changed its food into nutrients that plants can use. You might say that an earthworm is a living fertilizer factory.

A salamander chomps on a delicious, juicy worm. Earthworms, which are rich in protein, help nourish birds, frogs, snakes, and many other animals.

European and American freshwater eels are no ordinary fish. They look like snakes. They are as slimy as slugs. And by the time they are ready to mate they have finished an incredible journey from salt water to fresh water and back. Sometimes they even travel over land—up to two miles at a stretch.

These eels begin their lives in *salt* water in the Atlantic Ocean. They are born thousands of miles away from the streams, rivers, lakes, and ponds where they will spend most of their lives. When first hatched, they look like tiny, transparent willow leaves. They can't swim. Instead, they float along for one to three years. Currents carry them to the shores of western Europe and eastern North America.

When the eels arrive at the coasts, curious things begin to happen. They grow into their familar snake shape. Their skin begins to make its super-slimy coat. All fish have a coat of slime, or mucus. This coat protects them from infections and makes them slick so they can swim more easily. Eels just happen to have more mucus than most fish. Ask anyone who has tried to catch one.

Up to this point, all eels are the same. They are male and female rolled into one. At the coast, the eels split into two groups. Those that swim upstream eventually become females. Those remaining close to the coast become males.

Nothing stops the female eel in her journey upstream—and, several

Once eel larvae leave the ocean and enter freshwater streams and rivers, they turn into clear forms known as glass eels (above and right). As they swim upstream, they turn olive-brown. Years later, when ready to return to the sea, they turn black and silver.

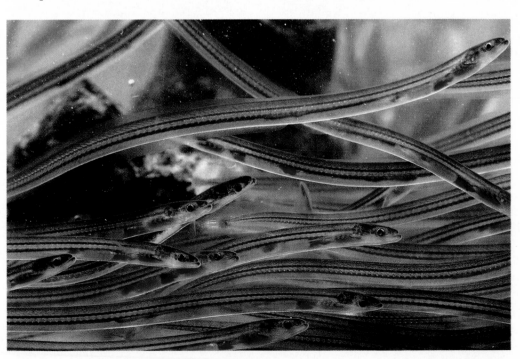

years later, downstream. She pushes up against rapids and squeezes between rocks. To get around a dam or to reach a land-locked lake, she may slosh through marshes, paddle in brooks, and swim through drains and sewers. Wriggling like a snake, she can also travel overland on rainy nights.

When the females are about fifteen years old, they begin their long journey back to the Atlantic Ocean. Males return to the breeding grounds when they are only six or so. The eels' journeys take three to five months. How they navigate is a mystery. Perhaps eels use their sensitive sense of smell.

No one is sure what route eels take on their return to the breeding grounds. Scientists do know that no eels have been caught in the open ocean. They also know that before the eels begin their journey "home," their eyes and swim bladders become more like those of fish that live deep in the ocean. From these clues, scientists believe that eels travel along the ocean floor.

Once they reach the right place in the ocean, the females release their eggs and the males fertilize them. Their duties done, the adults die. Tiny eggs soon hatch into tiny "willow-leaf fish," and the long, mysterious journey begins again.

A thick coat of slime keeps this adult eel from drying out as it wriggles across wet grass. Special gills allow the eel to breathe on land as well as in water.

It's a Snake!

Do you want to make someone jump? Just yell, "Look out! There's a snake!" Maybe the reason so many people are frightened by all snakes is because they can't tell poisonous ones from harmless ones. Or maybe it's because they think snakes look mean and aggressive or slimy and repulsive. Whatever the reason, a lot of people are afraid of these creatures. To them, snakes are the most unlovable animals of all.

But stop and think for a moment about how remarkable snakes are. Try to imagine what life would be like if *you* had to crawl everywhere, couldn't pick up your food, and couldn't close your eyes when you wanted to sleep. Snakes survive very well, and *they* have no legs, no claws, no ears, no eyelids, and no built-in way to keep themselves warm.

Like all snakes, this copperhead (above) uses its sensitive tongue and a special organ in its mouth to detect odors.

The rattlesnake (far right) adds a new rattle each time it sheds its skin, which can be up to three times a year.

Most snakes eat live animals—insects, worms, birds, frogs, and even other snakes. Capturing creatures that wriggle, run, or fly is never easy. Snakes have evolved a variety of ways to make sure their dinner doesn't get away.

Poisonous snakes use venom that paralyzes their prey. That's safer than trying to eat an animal that fights back. The U. S. has about 120 species of snakes, but only a few are poisonous. These are the rattlesnakes, moccasins, copperheads, and coral snakes.

Rattlesnakes, moccasins, and copperheads belong to a group of snakes called "pit vipers." These snakes have a small pit in the side of the snout between the eye and the nostril. The pit is sensitive to heat and reveals the presence of warm-blooded prey. A rattlesnake can detect a mouse more than a foot away in the dark.

After a poisonous snake strikes, the prey sometimes runs away. The snake doesn't chase it, though. The snake often patiently waits for the venom to take effect. It knows that its prey won't get very far.

Following a wounded animal is no problem for any kind of snake. Snakes have a very sensitive sense of smell. Like a person, a snake can smell with its nostrils. But it also follows scents with its forked tongue. When a snake flicks its tongue in and out, it picks up odor particles from the air or ground and

The red rat snake (left) is not poisonous. It preys on small birds and rodents like the white-footed mouse this one has caught.

If this caiman (below) looks a bit cramped, it's because every time it breathes out, the anaconda's coils tighten around it.

carries them into its mouth. A special organ there acts like a super-sensitive nose and tells the snake whether the scent is getting stronger or weaker. If the scent is stronger, the snake is closer to its dinner. Some people believe that a snake stings with its tongue, but that is simply not true.

Snake venom doesn't paralyze all animals. A common Virginia opossum is immune to some venom and eats rattlesnakes and water moccasins even when these snakes strike back in self-defense. King snakes, which are not poisonous, are also immune. That lets them feed on rattlers and other poisonous snakes. But if a rattler bites itself during the struggle, it may die from its own venom.

Sometimes a poisonous snake does not inject venom when it

strikes. Once a scientist working in Costa Rica was struck on the leg by a fer-de-lance, one of the most dangerous snakes in Latin America. The man waited and waited for the poison to take effect. Luckily, nothing happened. The snake was just trying to drive the man away. After all, he was too large for the snake to eat. That left the snake with venom to use when it did want to snag an animal for dinner.

King cobras are the longest poisonous snakes, measuring up to 18 feet or so in length. King cobras aren't the heaviest poisonous snakes, though. That title goes to the eastern diamondback rattlesnake of the southeastern United States. One of these snakes, just over 7½ feet long, weighed 34 pounds.

Though snake venom itself is dangerous, some useful things are

The egg-eating snake slowly works its jaws around an egg until the egg is swallowed (far right). It then breaks and spits out the shell (bottom right).

90

made from it. Doctors use substances found in venom to dissolve blood clots. Medicine made from cobra venom provides pain relief for people suffering from arthritis and cancer. A common use for venom is to make medicine to treat people bitten by poisonous snakes.

Snakes without venom have other ways of capturing their meals. Some snakes, for example, wrap themselves around their wriggling prey and squeeze. King snakes do this when they attack rattlers and other snakes. So do rat snakes when they catch mice and other small animals.

Few sights in the snake world are more impressive than the large squeezing snakes known as constrictors stretched out to their full length. Pythons in Southeast Asia occasionally measure more than 20 feet long, longer than a large car. Latin America's anacondas are almost as long, but they are fatter and weigh more. A 350-pound anaconda has little trouble capturing a small caiman, a reptile that looks like an alligator.

Male red-sided garter snakes are smaller than the females (above). In western Canada, these nonpoisonous frog-eating snakes huddle together all winter in their underground dens until mating season arrives in the spring. One den may hold 10,000 snakes. Finally, the warmer weather brings them wriggling out (right).

Boa constrictors in Latin America are the shortest of these snakes. They are rarely more than 15 feet long. Boa constrictors also have relatives in the western United States and Canada. But these shy snakes are real midgets and are less than two feet long. Both kinds, rubber boas and California boas, have a strange habit when bothered. They roll up into a tight ball.

Egg-eating snakes don't have to squeeze their prey or use venom. Eggs aren't going to fight back or run away. But these African reptiles still have two problems to overcome: how to swallow such a large meal and how to get rid of the shell.

An egg-eating snake's mouth is much larger than it appears at first glance. It has to be to stretch around an egg twice as wide as the snake's body. The skin around its mouth lies in flat folds, a bit like a closed accordion. When the snake eats, these folds open wider and wider until they reach all the way around the egg. Then hard bumps on the snake's backbone push in and break the shell.

To see an egg-eating snake in action, or any other snake for that matter, your best bet is to visit a zoo. Most snakes are shy and very difficult to spot in the wild. Their colors and patterns help hide them, and they *don't* chase after people.

It's wise to be alert for rattlers and copperheads when in the woods or for water moccasins when in the swamps. But don't worry so much that you are afraid to go to these places. Just watch your step and remember that more people in the United States are hit by lightning than are bitten by poisonous snakes.

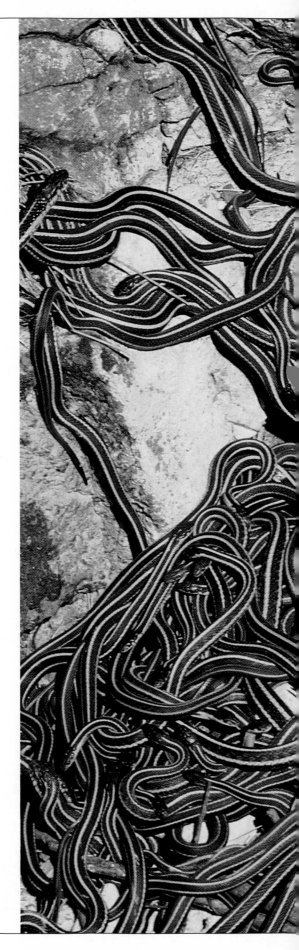

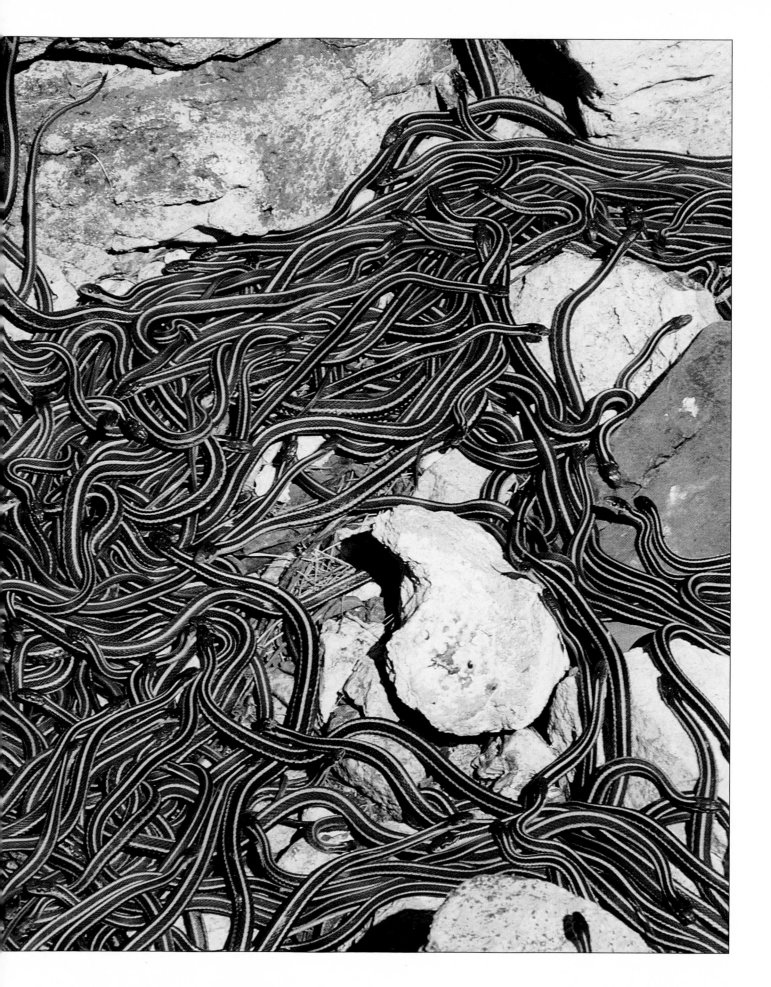

INDEX

Photographs are in *italic* type.

A

Africanized bee: (see Killer bee)
Alligator: 19, 20, *20-21*
Anaconda: *89,* 89, 91
Ant: 36, 81 (see also Fire ant)

B

Banana slug: 78, *78*
Bat: 64-67 (see also individual species)
Bee: 38, *40-41,* 41
Beehive: 41
Big-eared bat: 66, *66*
Black widow spider: 30, *30*
Blood: 52-54, 64-66, 68-69, 70, 72, 74-75
Blue-ringed octopus: 52, *54*
Boa constrictor: 94
Bolas spider: 34
Brown bat: 66
Brown recluse spider: 30
Bubonic plague: 22

C

Castings: 80, *80*
Centipede: 48-49, *49*
Cockroach: *44-47,* 45-47
Copperhead: 86, *86,* 92
Coral snake: 86
Crocodile: *18-19,* 19, 20

D-E

Dracula: *64*
Earthworm: 36, 48, 78, 80-81, *80-81*
Eel: 81, 82-83, *82-83*
Egg-eating snake: 90, *90-91,* 92

F

Fire ant: 36-37, *36-37*
Fire Ant Festival: *36*
Fishing spider: 34, *34*
Flea: 22, 74-75, *75*
Flea circus: *75*
Fruit bat: 66, *67*

G

Garter snake: 92, *92-93*
Glass eel: 82, *82*
Gorilla: 10, *10-15,* 12-13, 15
Great white shark: 56, *57,* 58
Grizzly bear: 24-27, *24-27*

H-I

Hammock spider: 34
Hammerhead shark: 56, 58
Horn shark: *58,* 59
Insects: 16, 36-41, 44-45, 65, 66 (see also individual species)

J

Jaws: 56, *56*
Jumping spider: 34, *35*
Jungle Book: 13

K

Killer bee: 41
Killer whale: 60-61, *61*
King cobra: 89
King Kong: 10, *10*
King snake: 89, 91

L

Leech: 68-69, *68-69*
Lemon shark: 59, *59*
Little Red Riding Hood: 6, *6*
Lyme disease: 74

M

Mako shark: 56, 58
Megamouth: 58
Mexican free-tailed bat: 66
Millipede: *48,* 48-49
Moccasin snake: 86, 92
Moose: 8, 9
Mosquito: 66, 70, *70-73,* 72-73
Mosquitofish: 73
Mucus: 76, 78, 81-82
Musk: 16

N-O

Nectar: 38-41, 66, 70-73
Octopus: 52-55, *52-55*

P

Pesticides: 37
Peter Pan: 19
Pods: 60
Poison: 22, 34, 42-43, 49, 52, 86, 89
Pollen: 38-41, *41*
Pupa: *73*
Python: 91

R

Rabies: 6, 65
Rat: 22-23, *22-23*
Rat snake: *88,* 89, 91
Rattlesnake: 16, 87, *87,* 89, 91-92
Red bat: 65, 66
Rocky Mountain spotted fever: 74

S

Salamander: *81*
Scorpion: 42-43, *42-43*
Shark: 56-59, *56-59* (see also individual species)
Silverback: 13
Skunk: 16, *16-17*
Slime: see Mucus
Slug: 78, *78-79,* 81-82

T-V

Snake: 47, 69, 82, 86-93, *86-93* (see also individual species)
Sonar: 60
Spider: 30-35, *30-35* (see also individual species)
Sting: 36, 38-39, 42-43

T-V

Tarantula: 30, *31*
Three Little Pigs: 6
Tick: 74-75, *74*
Tiger shark: 56, 58
Tularemia: 74
Vampire bat: 64-65, *64-65*

W-Y

Wasp: 38-41, *38-39*
Web: 28, *32-33,* 33-34
Web-casting spider: *33,* 34
Werewolf: 6
Wolf: 6, 8-9, *7-9*
Wolf spider: 34
Worm: see Earthworm
Yellow fever: 70

Cover, chapter openers, and all illustrations not otherwise credited are by Jean Pidgeon.

UNWELCOME VISITORS

6: top, *The Three Little Pigs* © 1933 The Walt Disney Company; bottom, Bettmann Archive. *7:* Scot Stewart. *8:* Jim Brandenburg. *9:* Paul E. Meyers. *10:* *King Kong,* copyright © 1976 by Dino DeLaurentiis Corporation, All Rights Reserved. Courtesy Paramount Pictures Corporation. *11:* John Cancalosi. *12:* Peter Veit. *13:* Norman O. Tomalin/Bruce Coleman Inc. *14-15:* Steve Solum/Bruce Coleman Inc. *16:* Stouffer Productions/Animals Animals. *17:* Breck P. Kent. *18-19:* Wolfgang Bayer. *19:* *Peter Pan* © 1952 The Walt Disney Company. *20:* Wendell Metzen. *21:* Stephen J. Krasemann/DRK Photo. *22:* Jane Burton/ Bruce Coleman Inc. *23:* Jane Burton/Bruce Coleman Inc. *24:* Jeff Foott. *25:* Stephen J. Krasemann/DRK Photo. *26:* Kennan Ward. *27:* Johnny Johnson.

CREEPY CRAWLIES

30: E. R. Degginger/Bruce Coleman Inc. *31:* Tom McHugh/National Audubon Society Collection/Photo Researchers. *32-33:* Ann Moreton. *33:* top, David P. Maitland/Auscape; bottom, David P. Maitland/Planet Earth Pictures. *34:* James H. Carmichael, Jr. *35:*

James H. Carmichael, Jr./ Bruce Coleman Inc. *36:* top, Stephen Myers; bottom, Courtesy of Greater Marshall Chamber of Commerce. *37:* Stephen Myers. *38-39:* Bianca Lavies. *40:* Christopher Morris/Black Star. *41:* Rod Planck. *42:* top, "The Far Side" cartoon by Gary Larson is reprinted by permission of Chronicle Features; bottom, Anthony Bannister Photo Library. *43:* top, Joe McDonald/ Animals Animals; bottom, P. Ward/Bruce Coleman Inc. *44-45:* Paul Phillip Sher. *45:* Raymond Mendez/Animals Animals. *46:* top, Chip Clark/Smithsonian Institution; bottom, Andrew Skolnick. *47:* top and bottom, Edward S. Ross. *48:* G. I. Bernard/Oxford Scientific Films/Animals Animals. *49:* top, Edward S. Ross; bottom, Robert W. Mitchell.

MONSTERS OF THE DEEP

52: Gary Milburn/Tom Stack & Assoc. *53:* Peter Scoones/Seaphot. *54:* Alex Kerstitch. *55:* all by Walter Lerchenfeld. *56:* Copyright © by Universal Pictures, a division of Universal City Studios, Inc. Courtesy of MCA Publishing Rights, a division of MCA, Inc. *57:* Marty Snyderman. *58:* both by Marty Snyderman. *59:* Peter Ward/Bruce Coleman Inc. *60-61:* Jeff Foott.

BLOOD LOVERS

64: Merlin D. Tuttle/Bat Conservation International. *65:* Gary Milburn/Tom Stack & Assoc. *66:* Merlin D. Tuttle/Bat Conservation International. *67:* Anthony Bannister Photo Library. *68:* top, Edward S. Ross; bottom, Russ Kinne/ Comstock. *69:* G. I. Bernard/Oxford Scientific Films/Animals Animals. *70-71:* both by Dwight R. Kuhn. *72:* top, Dwight R. Kuhn; bottom, Robert Noonan. *73:* top, Dwight R. Kuhn; bottom, Dwight R. Kuhn/Bruce Coleman Inc. *74:* top, Jeff Foott/ Bruce Coleman Inc.; bottom, Joe McDonald/Animals Animals. *75:* top, G. I. Bernard/Oxford Scientific Films/Animals Animals; bottom, Photri, Inc.

SLIMY, SQUIRMY, SLIPPERY

78: Jim Karageorge. *79:* Dwight R. Kuhn. *80:* Dwight R. Kuhn. *81:* Lynn M. Stone. *82:* both by Rodger Jackman/Oxford Scientific Films. *83:* John and Gillian Lythgoe/Planet Earth Pictures.

IT'S A SNAKE!

86: R. Andrew Odum/ Peter Arnold Inc. *87:* Breck P. Kent. *88:* Breck P. Kent/Animals Animals. *89:* Wolfgang Bayer. *90-91:* all by John Visser/Bruce Coleman Ltd. *92:* Brian Milne/First Light. *93:* Brian Milne/First Light.

Library of Congress Cataloging-in-Publication Data

The Unhuggables.

Includes index.
Summary: Describes the physical characteristics, habits, and natural environment of a variety of mammals, insects, and other animals people often fear, dislike, or simply ignore.
1. Animals—Miscellanea —Juvenile literature. [1. Animals—Miscellanea] I. National Wildlife Federation.

QL49.U54 1988 591 88-19531

ISBN 0-912186-91-7
ISBN 0-912186-96-8 (lib. bdg.)

Acknowledgements

Information included in this book came from a wide variety of scientific books and publications. In addition, experts in many fields offered insights into the anatomy and behavior of these odd yet fascinating creatures. Special thanks are due the following technical consultants. Each read one or more essays and offered detailed comments and recommendations:

Dr. Nancy Olds
American Museum of Natural History (New York)

Dr. Todd Newberry
University of California at Santa Cruz

Dr. Samuel W. James
Maharishi International University

Dr. Donald Messersmith
Dr. Geerat J. Vermeij
University of Maryland

Mr. Craig Phillips (retired)
formerly National Aquarium, Washington, D. C.

Mr. Ronald I. Crombie
Dr. Roy W. McDiarmid
Dr. Richard W. Thorington, Jr.
Dr. Kenneth A. Tighe
Dr. Stanley H. Weitzman
National Museum of Natural History, Smithsonian Institution

Dr. S. Douglas Miller
National Wildlife Federation

Dr. Michael H. Robinson
Mr. William A. Xanten, Jr.
National Zoological Park, Smithsonian Institution

Dr. Donald J. Klemm
U. S. Environmental Protection Agency

National Wildlife Federation

Jay D. Hair
President

Alric H. Clay
*Senior Vice President
for Administration*

William H. Howard, Jr.
*Senior Vice President
for Conservation Programs*

Francis A. DiCicco
*Vice President
for Financial Affairs*

Lynn A. Greenwalt
*Vice President
for Resources Conservation*

John Jensen
*Vice President
for Development*

S. Douglas Miller
*Vice President
for Research and Education*

Kenneth S. Modzelewski
*Vice President
for Promotional Activities*

Larry J. Schweiger
*Vice President for Affiliate
and Regional Programs*

Joel T. Thomas
General Counsel

Staff for this Book

Howard F. Robinson
Editorial Director

Victor H. Waldrop
Project Editor and Writer

Debby Anker
*Illustrations Editor
and Writer*

Elizabeth B. Blizard
Researcher and Writer

Donna Miller
Design Director

Holly Ritland
Designer

Jean Pidgeon
Illustrator

Michele Morris
Editorial Assistant

Paul Wirth
Quality Control

Margaret E. Wolf
Permissions Editor

Sandi Goldman Hettler
Kathleen Furey
Production Artists

Vi Kirksey
Christine Irwin
Production Assistants

NATIONAL WILDLIFE FEDERATION
1400 Sixteenth St., N.W., Washington, D.C. 20036-2266